"HELLO MY BIG BIG HONEY!"

"HELLO MY BIG BIG HONEY!"

Love Letters to Bangkok Bar Girls and Their Revealing Interviews

Collected by

Dave Walker & Richard S. Ehrlich

1992 First printing 1,000 copies
1992 Second printing 1,500 copies
1993 Third expanded edition 1,500 copies
1994 Fourth printing 1,500 copies
1995 Fifth printing 1,500 copies
© copyright 1992 by Dave Walker & Richard S. Ehrlich

Published by:
　Dragon Dance Publications
　Bangkok
　Thailand

Distributed by:
　White Lotus Company, Ltd.
　G.P.O. Box 1141
　Bangkok 10501

Cover photograph by Dave Walker

Printed in Thailand

ISBN 974-88761-9-5

An Introduction

By Dave Walker

The idea for this book began for me when a bar-owning acquaintance complained that he couldn't keep any bar girls because his customers kept marrying them. I remember thinking, "Love? In Patpong?" I never really imagined Bangkok's notorious bar district as a lonely hearts club or Asian marriage bureau.

Can one really find love among neon lights, touts, transvestites, pushers and VD clinics? Sometimes, the answer is yes. There are many foreign men who somehow do find true love in Bangkok's bars.

The love letters compiled in this book come from various countries. There are romantic letters from the French, German love letters full of Teutonic angst, and hundreds of letters from lonely men writing from cold, dull, passionless places where some have returned to a colorless, work-a-day reality after their holiday and fling in exotic Thailand. Many of the letters reflect desperate and sordid affairs in hotel rooms and squalid guest houses. Other letters are romantic and beautifully written.

What emerges are not-so-normal love stories and a very interesting look at human relations.

Among a bar girl's other occupational hazards—poverty, alcoholism, drug abuse, family problems, unwanted pregnancy, theft, betrayal, fights, VD, AIDS and arrest—comes love. Love, real or imagined, wanted or not.

Love is one four-letter word rarely mentioned in stories about Asia's sex industry. The relationships which develop between male customers and bar girls are as much a part of the story of Bangkok's sex industry as is AIDS, sex tours and all the "isms" that are prevalent and predictable in most feature stories on the bars.

This book explores those relationships through love letters donated by the bar girls and through in-depth interviews with a wide variety of the women involved. As well as the obvious financial advantage which a foreign customer has over the bar girl, there are many social and cultural pressures which the foreigner may not be aware of. These are explained in depth in the following pages.

Many of the women are surprised at how quickly foreign men seem to fall in love with them, and how many of these men become possessive and jealous after knowing them only a short time. For the bar girl, it's often just business as usual. For many men it's love.

It isn't difficult to see how a foreign man could fall in love with an Asian bar girl. They can be gentle, fun-loving, uncomplicated, slim and sultry. But they can also be cunning, ruthless and manipulative. There are many sad stories in Southeast Asia of both male and female victims of barroom marriages gone bad. Expats and tourists have lost their life savings to their Patpong dream girls or her scheming relatives. Barroom marriages can end in disaster for both the man and woman. Many of the women end up with alcoholics, drug addicts, unemployable drifters and worse.

Bar girls are loser friendly.

A foreign man coming to Asia is away from his day-to-day routine. He's in a strange new world. He's confronted by beautiful, available (for a price) exotic women who treat him like a king. For some, it's their ultimate fantasy. Any man, regardless of his looks or age, can become a popular playboy if he has enough money.

Many men like to think they're different from the other men in the bars. Some acquire a missionary-like complex, "I'll save this poor girl from this life of depravity," they think. The bar girls seem to like this kind of guy best as these are the types who usually send them the most money.

One of the misunderstandings which frequently occurs between bar girl and customer is the man's inability or unwillingness to send money to the woman's family. Sometimes her relatives pressure her for more money, thinking the foreigner is rich. What the man often fails to understand is that the girl's impoverished family comes first in her consideration, and that the girl will help her family by sending money home. The women are often supporting families and not supporting a pimp or crack habit like in many Western countries. In some cases, however, the bar girl is also supporting a husband or local boyfriend—unknown to the foreigner.

Some bar girls and foreign men do luck out. The transition from customer to boyfriend happens, they get married and the woman gets out of Patpong and settles down. Some women, however, return to the bars if the relationship fails. Many of the women have become hardened from too many broken hearts and promises.

Today, there are still few alternatives to back-breaking farm labor or tedious, menial jobs for poorly educated women. Bar work is one way out of the drudgery and poverty of rural areas.

The spread of AIDS and attempts by the government to scale-down prostitution has affected the bars. Patpong has mutated. Vendors selling trinkets have moved in, bringing tourists and bar-hoppers together. Touts shout in barely intelligible English with all the annoyance of barking dogs, trying to lure customers into expensive bars and sex shows.

"Hello My Big Big Honey!" is named after a love letter which inspired this book. This book does not intend to imply that the only Thai women foreigners meet and fall in love with are bar girls. This book focuses only on the relationships stemming from the bars on Patpong Road.

The analysis by Dr. Yos Santasombat whose brilliant insight into the relationship between bar girls and foreigners adds greatly to the letters and interviews. The epilogue by Mrs. Pisamai Tantrakul sums up the letters and interviews and helped us put the entire book in perspective.

The bar girls contributed their love letters as well as their support, trust, cooperation and humor for this book to give the accuracy we strived for. I thank them gratefully, because we couldn't have compiled this book without them.

To the men whose letters appear in this book, I thank you all for some fascinating material. May your love lives be positive and your blood tests negative.

I heartily thank my partner, photographer Satharn Pairaoh and my wife Praiwan for her patience and putting up with me, my bizarre projects and general eccentricity. Thanks also to "Blu" Gene Wallace and the expats at Blu Jeans Country Bar, Patpong Road for their comments and insight.

I also thank my co-conspirator Richard S. Ehrlich and his wonderful new Macintosh computer for helping pull this together. His skills as an interviewer are evident in the following pages.

An Introduction

By Richard S. Ehrlich

Bar girls live in a surreal nighttime world where men's fantasies, desperation, emotions and hormones collide with sleaze, partying, cash and intensive care. Often it's a raw transaction and no one looks back after they rise from the tangled sheets.

But like any place on this planet where boy meets girl, here in Southeast Asia's tropics among the carnival atmosphere and bars lining Bangkok's raunchy Patpong Road or along a quieter lane called Soi Cowboy or the myriad of other fleshy rendezvous—whoring sometimes tumbles into love. The odds are against it. When she's dancing on a tiny stage, a Thai bar girl might discover a row of men blandly watching her as if jurors at her trial. Or a man whose expression is so manged from years and fears that his face looks like a Rorschach inkblot which only she can interpret. In the shadows, a quiet drinker might be waiting for human balm for his antique body.

Her friends and competition will also be there, including the much too professional, pumped-up girls with their mercenary, split-level smiles beaming hot fake lasers of love. Other girls, jagged from smoking heroin or sniffing paint thinner or eating amphetamines, will scan the barroom with fierce, barbed-wire eyes unable or unwilling to conceal their own traumas. One girl's face might be pulled by invisible hooks into a frown as she numbly goes through the motions of dancing to the blare of "Like A Virgin." Other girls, gleefully laughing and trying to lure the crowd, will comically dance and strip. Some shows continue into crude cabaret.

Prostitutes have always driven some men crazy with love. Van Gogh may have chopped off part of his ear for a bar girl, though Van Gogh also threw his mind to the crows so he might not be an accurate measure of how deranged men can get when confronted by a female willing to pretend to be the answer to their dreams. Throughout human history, the oldest profession has inspired in some men eloquent poetry, opulent feelings and an honesty which can be lacking in the courtships, marriages and vows of other relationships. Much of the commercial intercourse in Bangkok, unfortunately, doesn't appear to be so lofty. Men are willing to pay, but they often quickly demand her sunny side up while the meter is ticking. Or kinkier acrobatics. And these days with AIDS, people on all sides are increasingly losing their lives.

But among the bars' clients and dancers are some foreign men and Thai women who are looking for love, though sometimes even they are unsure how to find it. Many of these infatuated men write love letters to their store-bought girlfriends. Even tonight, some Patpong women are carrying paper envelopes stuffed with hearts. This book is an attempt to take a look at some of these romances. In some cases, a gorgeous, sweet, stunningly erotic Thai bar girl is the indescribable explosion that a man suddenly sees as a faint glimmer of hope. Even though the customers usually return to their faraway nations, Bangkok becomes the place where they fall when they fall asleep.

Male chatter with their bar girls might be sexist, obscene, humorous, profound, scientific, pathetic,

10

disgusting or just a delight in the pleasures of the senses and a momentary illusion.

"Want me to write your name with a bottle of wine in the streets, to show you how I feel about you?" an American whispers to a lady on his lap. "Has anyone ever done that for you? Wasted a bottle of wine writing your name with it in the street?"

Or a German advises his buddy, "My best time was being with a squad of deaf and dumb hookers who were really nice because they never got on your nerves with silly talk. No talk about how you must marry them or anything."

Most customers don't fall in love, though many fall in lust. Some buy a purely physical thrill—affectionate, adept females who are more graceful, charming and beautiful than they have ever met. This book, however, focuses on those rare men who actually do plead to their girlfriends that their emotions are real.

The capital of Thailand is not unique as a place where men fall in love with ladies of the night. India caters to deprived romantics who can go to Bombay's so-called Cage District on Fauklin Road and search amid impoverished, beaten women dressed in ragged sarees and kept in a streetside zoo. In New Delhi, as night deepens, dank rooms fill up with stately nomad girls with thick dark circles drawn like black eggs around their eyes. They're camped in tents on the outskirts of the capital and sell themselves to rickshaw drivers, shoe shiners, peons and the male etcetera of the poor near the brick kilns and sandstone mines.

In Kenya, dilapidated Sunshine Clubs sometimes produce a black woman wearing a blonde wig to fill some kind of confused, modern need. Manhattan's Times Square mixes sex, dope and homelessness in a sort of illegal version of brutal free market enterprise. Amsterdam tries to pretty things up by placing its prostitutes behind glass windows so strolling pedestrians can peer into homey little rooms and view them like expensive merchandise.

This book portrays only a small group of people, limited to bar girls and their foreign boyfriends. There is, of course, an overwhelmingly larger community of normal romantic relationships in Thailand where people from foreign countries meet typical Thais and experience traditional, conservative courtship supervised by the family and leading to marriage.

Thailand and other areas of eastern Asia are, however, special in the way their bar girls inadvertently touch aspects of the Madame Butterfly syndrome where West sometimes meets East in a clumsy, fallacy-riddled way. A tropical girl speaking some kind of a beautiful, ancient bamboo language can quite easily hypnotize an innocent Western man abroad for the first time. Or the experienced foreign traveller might believe he can still rescue a promising Asian bar girl with his higher standard of living. As you read these pages, it may also sound like some of the women are surprisingly hip and have turned Madame Butterfly on her head, so the man ends up wailing on a distant shore as her personal automatic teller machine. Despite the confusion, missed cues and unlikely setting, such relationships and countless others often include feelings of love in both people. It is hoped this collection appears as a sort of opera, a stage for foreign men and Thai bar girls to display, in their own words, the elaborate way this love is sometimes born and how it tries to thrive against all sorts of impossibilities, real and imagined.

This book isn't an argument for or against the sex industry or a treatise on the miserable victimization suffered by many females who are forced by poverty, manipulation or need into selling their bodies. Other books examine those agonies. This collection tries to keep the focus on why so many foreign men fall head over heels for Bangkok's bar girls. Because of the swirling contradictions inherit in such uneven relationships, some of the letter writers will eventually taper off and cut the cord. Others, however, persevere believing—rightly or wrongly—that their love will change both of their lives and ultimately lift them from the mire.

I would like to dedicate this book to the women who gave letters and interviews to this collection. Good luck to all of you. Your voices are in these pages. I'd also like to thank Dr. Yos Santasombat for his elaborate, thoughtful prologue, and my colleague Dave Walker, for his investigative skills and enthusiasm.

Prologue

by Dr. Yos Santasombat

Dr. Yos Santasombat is an Associate Professor on the Faculty of Sociology & Anthropology at Bangkok's Thammasat University. He is also Research Director of the Local Development Institute in Bangkok's Department of Medical Science and author of the book, *The Community and Commercialization of Female Sexuality.*

Some of the points that I thought of when I read this manuscript, *"Hello My Big Big Honey!"* and of course also my own experience, is there are two categories of people: one is the girls themselves and one is the farang (foreigner), the clients or patron if we can put it that way.

Thai prostitution itself is, of course, very different from the West, and there are varieties of prostitution in Thailand as well. When you go to the brothel or hotel, it is one category of prostitution. But in Patpong or Soi Cowboy or Pattaya, you might find a different situation. And in the cases that are described in this book, it is more of what I would call a tourist-orientated, open-ended type of prostitution.

In this type of setting, there is a marked difference between the Western conception of prostitution, and the open-ended prostitution in Patpong or Pattaya. Because in the West, you see prostitution as an occupation. You go to them directly and then you strike a deal, and then you go straight to business. But in the case of Patpong, you see a lot of fuzzy areas in between the transaction.

The girls don't usually talk about the price at first. They would try to establish a rapport first. What the letters explain is that we're not talking about a piecemeal type of relationship that describes other forms of prostitution in the West. In the cases here, the Thai girls themselves are prepared to extend their relationship for a number of days or weeks or even years. Sometimes the farang himself ends up spending the entire vacation with one girl and sometimes he comes back. Sometimes she becomes his mistress or even a wife.

I think in most cases, the girls enter into the relationship from a strictly pecuniary motivation. But of course she may stage a concern in a sense of a physical attraction or some kind of an emotional attachment.

The girl will attach herself to a client or a farang more permanently if she finds the relationship enjoyable. Those are the cases I find most interesting in open-ended prostitution in Thailand.

Once the relationship is extended, the girls' involvement with the farang often gradually changes. Her stay with the man is usually conditioned upon his readiness to support her or to take care of her financially. The line between money and love becomes very fuzzy, because the money itself cannot be distinguished between signs of affection, tender caring and love itself. Mutual or material dependence frequently engenders some sort of an emotional attachment on the part of the girl herself.

So, what starts out as a money-orientated transactional arrangement becomes a mixed involvement, a more complicated relationship. In extreme cases it becomes even possible that the attachment comes from pure emotion. It somehow gradually detaches itself from the material aspects or the money. And in prolonged cases, open-ended prostitution can be characterized as an ambiguous compliment of love and money.

In the West, we talk about love and money as mutually exclusive. I don't think the same is true in open-ended prostitution here. The two cannot be separated or distinguished. It is much more complex in this regard.

What I find interesting in this book is the farang side of the whole thing. Somehow they are very naive, very stupid, sometimes very romantic. I feel both amused and sympathetic at the same time because the farangs themselves must be very confused when they enter into these relationships.

They are often not the most handsome of all, they are usually in the latter years of their life, they are bald, unattractive and quite lonely in their own little society. When they come to Patpong, they are struck with, first, not hard-core prostitution, not a deal, not the thing that they're accustomed to in the West, at home. But they are struck with girls who are all over them, who are trying to establish a relationship, and display physical attraction to them—which I think would be very confusing to a man in that position when they are not accustomed to receiving that kind of play.

So when the girls stage sexual interest or attraction to the farang, sometimes she may praise his good looks. In some case, who knows, the feeling may be genuine. And there is no talk about money in the first place. They will talk about his background, what kind of job he has, why he's here, if he has a family or not, something like that. Renumeration is never presented as a payment but rather as a reimbursement for lost income from the bar. It's always this trick that confuses the newcomer into this world.

The farang's sense of the world, his cognitive map, is thrown into chaos because he cannot make sense of what is going on in this deal. He cannot apply his concept of prostitution to the Thai situation. And he somehow would feel very uncertain whether a girl is with him for love or for money.

I think this question lingers on, even after he goes back home. Or even years after that. Especially if the relationship is extended for days or weeks or months, the farang is increasingly faced with the problem of meaning. How can he make sense of this relationship? What is the meaning of his relationship to this girl? Is she a good girl or a bad girl? This is a problem he has to confront all the time.

Some farangs try to convert the girl, try to rescue her from this hell hole and give her a chance to recover her own dignity, in a Western concept. This problem of meaning will continue to bother him for many years to come. He is in a kind of a dilemma. If he decides the girl is not a prostitute, and she continues to stay with him because she likes him, he wonders what makes him so attractive in the first place because at home, he usually never could find a girl, could not get a date, is shunned by the girls back home.

So, what is the difference between the girls here and the girls back home? Why are they attracted to him? Does he have some special qualities in him that the girls back home couldn't see? There are these questions that are coming up. But on the other hand if she stays on because of love, why does she always or insistently solicit money from him? So he is in a dilemma. The line between emotional commitment and material commitment is blurred in this type of arrangement.

Then, if she stays on for money, if that's the answer, then he wonders where her obvious enjoyment and her seeming attachment to him comes from. It seems genuine enough and in some cases it is. Some farangs might have tried to test her by refusing to give the girl the money she asked for, to see if she'll stay on, but only to be met with the girl's counter-gambit, namely the reproach that he doesn't love her enough because he refuses to help or support her. So he could not actually test her to the full limit of his capacity. So he can never solve this problem, this dilemma.

For some farangs who become more deeply attached to the girls after a prolonged relationship, they are, often as the letters have shown, after their departure, they are often worried about her fate, her destiny. And of course they end up writing anxious letters which reflect their concern.

But I also suspect from my previous research, these farangs might gradually transform. I think they will tend to treat the Patpong prostitutes more in an occupational, purely transactional arrangement. They'll try to avoid emotional relationships.

But in between the newcomers and old-timers, there are a lot of girls who are snatched and happily married, and who settle down elsewhere. Others become a mistress to these expats.

The farang side, to me at least, is more interesting and perhaps more difficult to understand in a way. We are facing here not only a subculture of Thai prostitutes, but we are talking about the French, the German, the Japanese, the Dutch, Americans, whatever. Each of these farangs have their own life experience, they have their own system of meaning. So, I don't think a similar letter which describes seemingly similar emotion means the same to each of these farangs. We have to be quite cautious not to assume they all share the same experience and the same meaning with the Patpong prostitutes because they have different backgrounds, they have different preconceived ideas about what an emotional relationship is all about. So the farang side is much more complicated, much more problematic in a way.

Thai women always have their roots which lie much deeper in her family. She feels a sense of family obligation, a need to support the family which I think also bewilders the farangs because Western prostitutes seldom talk about their families. In the West, they will use the money for drugs or whatever, but seldom for the family.

Probably the farang newcomer will hear for the first time about a girl needing money to buy a buffalo or to pay the mortgage, or whatever, for her family. I think that would throw him into lingering doubt thinking, "What is going on here? Why is she here in the first place? So, she is not doing this on her own? She is doing this against her will in a way, because she has to?"

So a moral judgement is cast in the first stage that, "OK, she's doing this for moral reasons. So, immoral practice for moral reasons is good, it's acceptable. So I should be a missionary now trying to save her from this misguided trap that she's in. So I'll pull her through and try and get her to become 'straight' in a Western concept."

For those very sloppy, unattractive males, this would become even more of a great opportunity for them to strengthen their macho ego. They can think, "I am sexually attractive! For the first time in my life I am sexually attractive! I have a beautiful girl who has become very attached to me, loves me, cares for me." There is a sense of wanting to give, to help in a way.

When a newcomer walks into Patpong, he is usually approached by a more experienced girl. A new girl would not dare to approach a farang in the first place. So he is now at a very disadvantageous position because he is dealing with someone who has been through this for quite a number of years. She can stage a great deal of her past experience on him, show her attraction to

19

him, establish a very good relationship with him, and give him all the tricks of the trade.

But once a relationship is prolonged, if he shows he really cares, if he could be a potential supporter, if the relationship is quite enjoyable, then it is quite usual for the girl to develop a real sense of interest. Not only for the money itself, but also for security.

The prostitutes always look for a catch because they know they can't do this for a living for many years. Once they hit 30, they are in the bottom of a barrel. They have to find a way out. Either by saving the money, which is much more difficult to do, or to get a good catch. Get married. Marry the foreigner.

Marrying a Thai would be impossible. She could get a taxi driver or a coolie who will be more of a burden to her than be a supporter. So a search for a real companion, a real supporter, is always in the back of these girls' minds.

If she could develop a genuine relationship with a farang, if he shows signs of interest, of caring, of becoming a good supporter, I think the chances are these girls will fall into the trap—an emotional relationship. Obviously these things do happen very often. But of course in many cases, the girls fell in and out of love so many times that they have less and less hope that they could find Mr. Right Guy.

Those girls who are in the middle—not so experienced, but have enough experience to solicit the attention of a farang newcomer, and attract and develop mutual affection—end up going away and getting married. As this book's findings show, they do get married very often and they disappear from the market. So it means some of these relations work out.

When you enter a relationship with a Thai woman, you are not getting into an individual unit of experience. You're getting into a family relationship. When you marry the girl, you not only marry her, you marry the family.

You cannot separate and take her out of that unit of experience and expect her to respond only to you and you only to her. That is not possible. You now have to deal with her father, her mother, her aunts, uncles, so on and so forth. And if you are potentially in a position of wealth or could become a supporter, then you will be bombarded with requests by family members who expect that you also have an obligation to help them. If you are not prepared to shoulder all those responsibilities, you have to go back. This is true not only with a good girl but, as is described in this book, it also happens with the prostitutes as well.

Another difference is, in the West you don't usually give money to the girl as a gift or present. You can buy her an expensive present—which means exactly the same thing because you spent the same amount of money on her—but the girl will tend to think this is not money, this is a token of love, of affection.

But the Thai girl would think otherwise. You give her the money, and it's the same as when you give her an expensive gift. She doesn't think of money as having a derogatory connotation. But in the West, you can't do that. It would be misogynist behavior, a patronizing male ego to give money to the girls. But here, the girls expect support from males.

It is different now with middle class Thai women. They tend to remain single, thinking, "If you can't get a good catch, better not get it at all." So, many of them remain single for the rest of their lives. It's getting much more difficult for a middle class girl to find a boyfriend out of school or university, so they have become more achievement orientated in the past decade. They tend to look for a higher qualification in their partner. They don't have to be dependent upon a man.

So they turn their aggression inward and are more aggressive in their work. After a while, she misses the train, she can't go back and catch it. After 30, it is almost impossible for a girl to get married. It's very, very difficult.

I'm not saying there are more single middle class girls than married ones, but I think the number is on the rise. They're looking for a Thai companion, a friend, but they end up having a dominating, self-serving partner. Once they can separate themselves from a position of having to depend on someone—for instance when they are self-sufficient—they start to ask questions, "Why do we have to get into this relationship?"

It is well known, and I think most Thai men will not admit this, but I do, that the majority or a great number of Thai men are quite irresponsible as compared to women. And it has historical explanations to this. The Thai family is a female-centered system, so it consists of women who are always there, from the grandmother to the mother to the daughter.

The relationship is very close and along the female line, while the men come and go. The men would be recruited into the army for two years—or even more when, in the old days, they still had to fight the battles— or they are recruited into coolie labor or they usually go elsewhere all the time. But it is the women who are there, they work in the field, raise the children, they shoulder all the economic aspects of running the household.

It is also partly because of women's attitude towards boys or sons—they prefer to have sons—that men are spoiled brats. Because Thai mothers feel a son will bring her a Buddhist yellow robe once he gets ordained as a monk and he can give her a great deal of religious merit and all that. So in terms of traditional values, sons are much more pampered than girls. Girls are trained to be responsible, running the household, how to work in the fields, how to cook, while men know very little about these things.

I've been telling the feminist groups in Thailand is what you need most is to re-educated the Thai male. Give them some sense of value. I think this is very important.

In northern Thailand, a prostitute can sometimes go back home and get married to a fellow villager. Of course there are reasons for this. He gets a lot of fringe benefits from the money that she has saved up, or from her land. This is well-accepted in the north.

But in the northeast, this is still very problematic. She would be stigmatized and she could be the focal point of gossip and a mockery of her village. So northeasterners usually don't make it known to their friends and their families that they are prostitutes.

In contrast, northern Thai girls can go directly from their villages to a massage parlor or a brothel and they are openly accepted back in their own villages. I don't think northeasterners are willing to accept that with the girls. For the northeasterners, there's a lot of networking of people who are seasonal migrants, who come to Bangkok to sell food, and are in all the other trades.

They have village-specific groups or networks that links people from different provinces. When they come from the same province, from the same district, they know each other, they help each other out. So once a girl from a particular place is found to have become a prostitute, it is quite difficult for her. Marrying a foreigner is the best option left to her.

I think in the northeast, very little pressure is being put on the girls for them to bring home money. In the north, the pressure is enormous but not so much because the parents want them to go, but because of their elder sisters, their peers, their friends show them the success cases.

So they want to imitate this success. They want to have the money. They want to look so beautiful like the girls who have been in Bangkok for a year, those who go back to their village and are beautiful. So the girls see all these successful cases and they want to have the same. They want a new house, a car, a lot of money to spend. So the pressure from their family hardly matches the pressure from the examples they see, from their friends.

In the north, you can't explain prostitution in terms of poverty. Because how do you define poverty in the first place? If you define poverty as having nothing to eat, that's not really true in the north. But if you define poverty as not having a motorcycle, or a pickup truck, a color TV, a video tape, then you get into a whole new situation.

In northern Thailand, the majority of the prostitutes begin because they want to become a modern consumerist. They want a chance—equally, or as much as the middle class girls—to consume as much as they want. So in a way, it is this commercial culture, consumerism, that has driven them into betraying themselves. In the northeast, it is a mixture of poverty and consumerism.

In the northeast, the pressure can be from real poverty because northeasterners are much poorer than the north. Subsistence agriculture is no longer a viable alternative. Seasonal migration comes into view here. Small-scale enterprises, vendors, hawkers are popular alternatives for northeasterners.

Examples from the years of the American G.I. presence in Udorn, in Ubon, in many northeastern towns, show them they can make quite a bit of money if they become, not a prostitute, but a hired mistress "mia chow"—a word preferred by northeasterners instead of "prostitute."

In Patpong or elsewhere, when you find a majority of the girls are from the northeastern or the central plain, there is a sense of identity quite separate from the other prostitutes. Northeastern girls tend not to think of themselves as full-fledged prostitutes. They would jokingly call themselves "entertainer" or "service girls" or "dancer."

If Western men, learning about Thailand from popular magazines or tourist agencies' advertisements, feel that they can come and buy their way for a few hours, a few days, of good time in the so-called sex industry, I think they are in way over their head. They don't know what they are getting. They're not prepared for the years of mental trauma and emotional upheaval that some of these letters have expressed.

I think they come with a very superficial view of what reality is all about. Once they are faced with the enormous complexity of the situation and the enormous amount of problems they are not equipped to solve, then they are getting into a great deal of headache. So they go away with part of them still being here. Instead of having a good time—sometimes they'd have a good time—but they go away leaving something, leaving much more of their desires still in Patpong which is not a very nice place to leave part of yourself.

From the letters you see the proof of the attachment, this longing for affection, for love that they previously got from Patpong and not, unfortunately, from their own country, from their own society. So, in a search for a few days of good time, they end up with emotional torment for many years. Is it worth the money that you had saved up? I think this is the question that the farang has to ask before they come to Thailand.

They are not ready to face this complexity, this emotional burden that they will have to shoulder for many years to come. Or don't they think they will face this problem, this dilemma? I think most of them don't feel this way. Most of them don't think they will have this kind of a problem, and they go away having these problems for many years.

The number of prostitutes in Thailand range from 300,000 to one million. It depends on which sources you want to believe. In the whole sex industry, about 65 to 70 per cent are from the north. About 30 per cent come from the northeast or from elsewhere. But I suspect in Patpong, or Soi Cowboy, or in Pattaya, the majority come from the northeast. Perhaps because of their darker complexion and their sense of not being the attractive type in terms of the Thai concept of beauty, they feel they would have more appeal to the Westerners.

And maybe it's true, because I have been talking with a lot of mama-sans and they say northeastern girls do much better with the foreigners than northern girls. Perhaps because newcomers prefer more aggressive women. The girls from the north tend to be shy and keep to themselves. So northeastern girls get more clients than the northern girls.

Thai men tend to laugh at Patpong and look at it as some stupid farangs spending their money with what they consider the ugly women in Patpong. The category of women in Patpong would not fit their image of beautiful women in Thailand. And these women are very rude, very up-front which is not a manner that a Thai would subscribe to as respectable. So in a way the women and the farangs are there because both of them want to be there, and they are free to do so if they see fit.

I think these are the real questions involved when we ask, "Why are these girls there?" We have to talk about the gradual disintegration of farming communities. We have to talk about the expansion of the bottom level of society. The poor gets poorer, in a way, and why is that happening?

It has much more to do with the culture of survival in a way, that there is no moral judgement, or moral system that could be applied in this direction. When you talk about morality to these women, there are many aspects of morality. They will say they are doing a wonderful job of raising their young sisters and brothers so what's wrong with that? What's wrong with selling what they already have? And I find it's very difficult to argue with them. I find that morality is not an issue here. And when you talk about it in terms of pure business matter, it's not even applicable too. It's more of partly a welfare system, partly an entertainment system, partly to find a better life for themselves. They are a future-orientated group of women. So, it's very difficult to categorize them which would grasp the whole meaning of their existence.

For the lower class, the question is not the inequality of the sexes. Both sexes are exploited. You have the male filling the vacuum of cheap labor. And you have the female filling the vacuum of the sex trade. So both male and female are exploited.

Technical Details

The following letters and interviews were given by bar girls in Bangkok. Women were asked for whatever love letters they had received from foreign men, and to tell about their lives. We rejected hundreds of letters and many of the interviews and selected only the ones which were interesting or displayed emotions.

It was impossible for us to find out the fate of many of these relationships. Often the women themselves didn't know why they drifted apart. Sometimes the women were about to travel to join their foreign boyfriends.

To protect everyone's privacy, we changed every bar girls' name to "Darling" and all letter writers' names were deleted. To ensure anonymity, we also deleted descriptions of the men's jobs and removed the names of all foreign cities, substituting instead the name of the country. All dates were also deleted or replaced by "soon" or "recently."

In the few cases where writers kept mentioning their own names in the text of the letter, and their names became intrinsic to the letter's cadence and mood, we simply replaced their real names with two invented names: Hubert and Floyd.

The sometimes twisted grammar in the letters are the exact text—we corrected their typos and misspellings—and we only used letters which were written in English. The letter writers' attempts at Thai phrases are translated in a glossary.

Dave relentlessly searched the bars to find letters and interviewees.

I, meanwhile, interviewed the women. I concentrated on those who spoke relatively good English, and I transcribed their replies verbatim.

The bar girls I interviewed do not match up with every published letter. This is because many of the bar girls who gave Dave fascinating, romantic letters, were not always the most eloquent or lucid interviewees. Similarly, some of the best interviewees declined to let their more intimate letters be made public — or simply never saved them.

The statistics are also a bit random: some women had only one letter worth including, while others received a handful of collectables. To ensure confidentiality, we also jumbled the published order of the letters and interviews so no one reading the book would be able to identify which women received which letters.

In this expanded edition, we added a new interview I did with a mama-san who helps manage one of the bars on Patpong Road. From her unique position overseeing the hiring, conduct and complaints of women working in her bar, she describes the behind-the-scenes activities which bar girls must endure on the job, and the consequences falling in love sometimes has for them and their customers.

GLOSSARY

Ab nam	take a shower or bath
Baht	Thai currency, divide by 25 to get U.S. dollars
Butterfly	slang for a person who sleeps around
Cheap Charlie	cheapskate
Chuk wa	literally "pull the kite," slang for masturbate
Don Muang	Bangkok international airport
Farang, falang	foreigner, usually spelt farang
G.I.	general infantryman in the U.S. Army
Ganja	marijuana
Hua Hin	a beach resort
Juk jik	slang for scatterbrained girl
Khow pat moo	"rice fried pork"
Koh Samet	island resort near Bangkok
Koh Samui	island resort in southern Thailand
Kuay	slang for penis
May Law	not handsome
Men	bad smell
Mekong	Popular Thai whiskey, named after the river
Noy	common Thai girl's name
Pat prio wan	"fried sour sweet"
Patpong Road	Bangkok's famous red-light district
Pattaya	nearby beach resort

Petchburi Road	where a cluster of bars and night-clubs were in the 1960s, popular with American soldiers on leave during the Vietnam War
Phuket	another island resort in southern Thailand
Pratunam	a Bangkok neighborhood
Sabai sabai	"comfortable"
Sanuk	fun
Sawadee	greetings
Smack	heroin
Suriwong	a hotel near Patpong
Taleh(or "dolae")	tell a lie
Tchak waho	an alternate spelling of chuk wa
Teelak, or tee rak	darling
Tuk tuk	three-wheeled, golf cart-style taxi
V.D.O.	video
Yat	cousin

BRITISH AIRWAYS
flying between _____
and _____
First Class

Darling,

I am writing to you on the aeroplane because I want my letter to reach you as quickly as possible.

I will try to write in very easy English so your friend can tell you what I say in Thai.

I (Hubert) was very, very sad to say goodbye to you this morning at Don Muang (airport). Like you, Hubert also cry. But do not worry, Hubert will come back to see you very soon. I will try to come back to Bangkok to see you soon. I think I can stay for about two (2) weeks next time.

I want to tell you so many things. I feel very bad on the aeroplane because I miss you already. Also, I feel very angry because I cannot write to you in Thai. Sorry.

I want to say very big thank you for coming with me to the airport (Don Muang). I know it was very sad time for you (and sad for Hubert too), but Hubert was very pleased with you and very proud of you for being very brave.

I will try to help you with money. But please do not expect too much from me—because now I have to save money to come to Bangkok again soon.

I will write to you again to tell you how much I have (money) in the bank. Not very much I am sorry.

I was very pleased to give you the little presents (gifts). I will send you some more little things soon.

Now comes more important words:

VERY IMPORTANT AND "TOP SECRET"

I wish I had met you as soon as I came to Bangkok. We did not have enough time together. But I really enjoyed your company and Hubert feel very good with

32

you. I think you are very good-looking (very pretty) and, first of all when I see you dancing, I am very attracted to your lovely, young body (very sexy!)

But, as we spent more time together, I start to think darling is a lovely person. You are fun to be with and have good heart. I really enjoyed taking you to places and you make old Hubert feel very young again. I say old Hubert. Please understand darling that Hubert is in his forties. Old enough to be your father! What do you think of that? Perhaps you think that Hubert is a "dirty old man" to have sex with a young lady (you). Hubert felt very good to make love to you, but because you are much younger, sometimes old man Hubert find it difficult to please darling. You have so much energy. This is why I say (joking to you) "Doctor, Doctor, please save me, give me some medicine (vitamins) so I can make love again to my darling."

No joking now.

Making love is good now and again and I hope you enjoyed it too. But there is more to life than making love. I think we became very good <u>friends</u> and I hope I will always stay a good friend to you. You speak only little bit of English and I speak only little bit of Thai but I think we are very good for each other.

I was sad when you tell me you have no mother and no father in Bangkok. Do your mother and father die? Please tell me about your family, I would like to know more about you.

なな なな なな

Dear Cuddlee Wuddlee,

Sorry I do not write back before but your letters take a long time to get to me. One letter took 2 weeks + to get to me—have you got problem with post in your country?

33

Why do you cry and drink beer? You know I only joking—I say butterfly because I not hear from you for long time and I <u>worry</u> too much about you. OK I stupid to say that and I'm sorry—I know you are good girl and I trust you <u>100%</u>. So if I say something in letter please don't take me too seriously—often I speak in letter same as if you were sitting next to me and I joke—you know I often say something, then smile when I know you little bit angry and are going to hit me—it's the same; when I write letter it's as if you are with me. So stop your crying Yat sister!!!!

So I send you 4 really great photos and all you say is P.S., your whole letter is about Butterfly!!! Boring! In your letter tell me more about yourself and what you think of my family, how all my friends in Thailand, where we shall go when I come back.

I very angry: I send long long letter just after Christmas—I write many many pages and my brother write letter and I send little money £10—430 baht approx. I'm pissed off—someone stole it—at post office or at your house.

Listen, I think of you all the time and not have farang girl so shut up!!!! Could get farang girl but do not want. I dream of you very much and want to cuddle you, hold you, kiss you and make love to you all day and all night. When I'm inside you nothing else matters, I want you so much—all I have is my pillow and "chuck wa"!!!!

I want you look after your body for me; if you love me you <u>stop</u> smoking, <u>stop</u> drinking, and not ride motorbike. You have lovely skin—I don't want you to have cigarette burn on your leg like before from Patpong, and please I don't want your lovely legs to get vein in them from smoking, and your feet to get hurt from dancing in high-heel shoe. Tell me—are your legs still beautiful?

34

TAKE CARE YOUR BODY !!!!

Also, I worry about you so much because over in my country all I hear is about AIDS—all the time. People are really worried about it here, it is killing lots of farang—mostly lady-men (Gay men) who fuck up the ass and people who inject drug—you know with needle in arm. But also beginning to spread through man and women who fuck normally. I so worried about you my darling. I am crying now myself! I know you clever girl, I know you good girl, I know you use condom every time but still I worry because condom not 100% safe.

If you go with man, always go with shy man—man who has not been in Patpong before. Virgin men!! No, I silly but good man older man who not fuck or worst of all use drugs—99% sure of getting AIDS when go with man who use needle in arm like your girlfriend did once—you remember her come back from man who use heroin. Also make sure you have good AIDS test doctor—go to hospital and not bullshit doctor who is no fucking good and always make sure when you get AIDS test the doctor never use same needle as another person.

When you write back tell me you have good AIDS test and Doctor. God I worry too much about you.

But best of all my darling: Listen. Please please get out of Patpong. I know it is hard and you have to send money for your son. If you need to get teeth done I will send you money so have nice teeth—£70 I think you said—that is OK. When I come back Thailand I want you out of Patpong—how do you think I feel—my girlfriend going with other men. Its not right. Also my brother working very hard, he is saving all his money and wants to come travelling with me to Thailand. I would like you to meet me off plane. But what am I going to tell him? Also I want you to meet my friend one day. What do I tell him? And what about when we

35

go on holiday again have I got to pay fucking bar 3,000 baht just to go on holiday with you for a week. Your boss is a fucking wanker—you can tell him that from me. Any man who makes money out of young girls selling their bodies is cockroach (Malang Sap). OK I shut up now but think about it. When I come back to Thailand I want my baby out of Patpong, and in good job. Try darling please.

Answer all my questions. In your next letter don't just say "You not worry about me", or "I love you forever"—write me long letter answering all my questions and don't be sad or angry because you know I love you. OK. Cuddlee Wuddlee.

Write me a letter as soon as you get this—don't go Ab Nam or get Coca-Cola from shop or watch video with your girl friend!!! OK shut up now Cuddlee Wuddlee

Not long now before I come back. I am working hard, earning lots of money and will be back Thailand soon. I could come in sooner but this time I bring more money—I want to bring 100,000 baht to keep me going long time. My plan is to do course and learn to speak Thai very good and then to write Thai!!! With 100,000 baht I can stay in Bangkok more than a year without working. Then when I can speak well can get good job teaching English—more money better job then if I cannot speak Thai language well.

What do you think—good idea? So don't worry the time will soon go and before you know it you'll be cuddling me airport and riding in Tuk Tuk and then what I want is to go Chiang Mai with you—we fly in aeroplane! Hurry and send me a tape—but not if too expensive to send to England. And what I would really like is for you to teach me some new words—say word in English and then Thai—do you understand my baby? Keep learning English better! I still remember all the

words I learn before in T/L—I'm not crazy man !!!!!!!!!
Write soon. Love you lots. Tell me if you still love me.
I know you do but I like when you say. xxxxxx

~ ~ ~

Darling,

My head is in Thailand and my body in France. My
life is like that. Every day I listen record of Thai song I
buy alone the last night in Patpong when you stayed in
Pattaya.

I am so happy last time, to see you again. Sometime I
don't understand what you don't understand.
Nevermind. It's so big happiness to know you and try
to be OK with you and to have good time with you

I'll go back in Bangkok soon, perhaps with my wife.
Don't worry for you, my wife is a very good girlfriend
like you. I think you can understand.

Did you open an account in the Thai Farmer Bank
like you tell me last time? If you want I send you
money, you need to open account.

Bye-bye my pretty darling. See you again soon (I stay
only 2 days).

~ ~ ~

Darling,

In my flat, I have a big Buddha, I buy it near the
Ramada Hotel, I'm very happy to have him because I
can do meditation often.

Are you making meditation too?

I hope so because it is fantastic, just for that, it was
important to be in Thailand, it changed me, and now I
think I'm on the right way or better way than before.

It's coming late and I would like to sleep, maybe you want to come in my dreams!

It's sure that I want to write you again and quickly. I give you many many many kisses and all my heart.

ða ða ða

Darling,

I am sending $200 to your account at Bangkok Bank. You will have the money when you read this letter. I want you to use it to study more or to save for your future. Remember it is for <u>your</u> use.

I hope you are well and happy. I will see you soon. I will write you another letter before then, to tell you exactly when I will arrive and on what flight. I am anxious to see you again.

<u>Please write me a letter</u> when you get this one, to let me know that you have received the money. I hope you are still studying English so we can communicate better in the future!

I hope your job is going well and that you can do even better when the tourist season begins. I miss you!

Love.

ða ða ða

(She resides upstairs in a bleak building typical of many bar girls' living quarters. A ceiling fan churns humid air which smells of food cooking on a hotplate placed on the floor in the hallway. She has shiny, pink toenails, and six finger-rings, some of them gold. Her elderly mother, who is emaciated and extremely wrinkled, comes in from the bathroom topless and puts on shirt. The bar girl points to her mother and boasts, "Sexy!" Her mother gives a toothless smile and departs.

Dust-covered cobwebs dangle and sway in the ceiling's corners and the room is sectioned off by turquoise-painted plywood. Someone has rubbed purple lipstick all over the mouth of a young Thai actor in a big poster. Another poster shows a larger-than-life baby. Five people share the bedroom—which is little bigger than the bed— two children, the bar girl's sister, the sister's boyfriend and a girlfriend. In the only other room, she sleeps with her son and mother near a VCR and dart board. As she speaks, a nude baby boy sleeps on his back on the bed. The room's floor is covered with thin, roll-down linoleum. On a top shelf rests a gray, stuffed animal with its eyes missing.)

(what do you think of the letters you receive?)

Too sweet. All letters be sweet. One German write, also he do send money. He very good. Other man forget about me because just like to make letter and after never heard about again. I like this German because he very good, he young but have very good thinking. I never see anyone German like him. I like him, him good care, good love, not butterfly. Two years I know him. I never love him, only like him. It hurts too much and is too scary to love him. Because the first one hurt me really bad, from England. German love me too much.

(do you believe his letters?)

I do. About future, I talk to him already. If I marry I want to stay Thailand because have too much to take care. My family. My mother, my son. The town of my boyfriend is not in the city and is very boring, like in the village. I went Germany two times. I like him family, very good care of me. I don't think so I like Germany, too cold for me. He say, "OK," but he also will like to stay Thailand but difficult him. Because he don't have job. Now I 27. Old? I from Bangkok. I worked Patpong but I don't like. I don't like show people my body in go-go bar. When I dance, I have to be drunk first so I not shy to do it. Some girl she not too much like, but she have to do it. Because Thailand difficult to find job. Girl come from everywhere. It not easy. You want a job. My whole family work in carpenters. Difficult. (laughs) Not my style. Very hard work, very tiring. Take a long time for my mother to know what I doing.

(why are you a bar girl?)

A lot of farang ask why because they never give mother money. But all Thai people, tradition when mother get old we have to give back. Two, three years she know my working. She can say nothing. How she can say? Because I doing already. First she feel not good. She think why, why you have to go this way? But she feel nothing because my auntie marry with a farang more than 10 years. I go to learn English. Three months. I have to learn. Take a long time. Before, very funny. I have one dictionary I carry with me. When farang ask me, I have to look in dictionary. This guy I know him two years, he always take care of me, more than enough. I pay the room, give every month for my mother 5,000 baht because she take care my son too.

(what are your total monthly expenses?)

More than 10,000 baht.

(is being a bar girl good or bad work?)

Maybe good, maybe no. Because girl always come Bangkok, find job, and can work here and maybe good for her future. But now have too much girls working. Man he marry me, I don't care rich or not. But only one thing: he can take care of me and my family. Some girl work two year, she get fun, she get crazy. Crazy like she think when she still have life, she have good time. Because she can see a lot of things, she can know everything. She can see, can learn how heart is hurt, like broken heart, sometimes she can see how she can be fighting for everything. Can be crazy about first the man good care, then after he leave then he forget. She hurt and make her crazy. Thai people when we stay with one person, good care. She think about future to be with this guy but the guy only think pay to her one, two year and forget. Always say to the girl, "Love you," but when he going back he forget. Write letter only for one year. I find older men good for me. He like me because I intelligent girl, control myself, when I talking have a brain like a woman talk. When we stay together we can be friends, sometimes like a brother, like we know for long time. Older man he don't forget me.

(what is the difference between men from different countries?)

Different country, I think all think the same. Some very good, but some very crazy. For me I don't care about the country. The farang are the same type of people, have to work hard. I marry with a husband went to England. I think not different than my country. One thing is he can find a good job, not like in Thailand. And if can't find job, government can take care him, not like in Thailand. I marry with him about five years, but now not together. Very funny I meet him. I come to bar to drink and see him stop motorbike and he ask me, do you know what he ask me? "Have ganja?" I said, "What you think I like that?" And he say, "You look stoned."

41

(why did you separate?)

Always fighting. He crazy. The problem was he too much jealous because I open the bar I have to take care customer, I have to keep talking. But he don't understand. He think I have to go with the man. He buy the knife, (laughing) tell the customer, "You can speak with my wife but can't touch her." I never tell customer I have a husband, because the business, so I keep talking. After he buy the drink, he think this bar very good and he come again. I have son.

(who is the father?)

I don't want to say. First time you work you don't know from who. Now he's around six years old.

(are you worried about AIDS?)

A lot of people care about it. We can know about it. All girls talk. A lot of men don't like condom. If use condom, man say, "Very different, cannot make it." I tell my girlfriend, "You have to be careful."

(any advice to a new girl who is thinking about starting as a bar girl?)

Working this not good. Better she can find the other job. I think the old girl is better than the young, because young think work for fun. But old girl think how to get money tonight to pay tomorrow, not work for fun. I think next year I going to get married to him. Then I only live Germany one year, but not for life. But if I can find a job there, I stay there because Thailand make me crazy. When I go with farang in Thailand I never hold hand, I let him walk ahead because many Thai people don't understand why Thai girl go with farang.

❧ ❧ ❧

Dear little Darling,

It seems so long since I saw you last and every day I want to take a plane to Bangkok to see you, but I have too much work in Belgium now and I cannot come.

I miss you very much, too much!

I am living here with my girl-friend, but I think of you all the time and I don't want her, I want you!

I think too much and I want to have you with me all the time.

I wanted to send some money to Bank but it is very difficult, so I put in this letter some money.

I would like to send you more so you don't have to work so much, but it is not possible, maybe next year if my work goes well I can send enough money so that you don't have to go to work any more and so that you can take classes in English and Thai.

I know you don't like to receive money from me but it is better from me than from someone else.

I don't know what to say as I will sound very stupid, but I don't care—I really care only about you and I really hope I can take care of you very soon—I want to make you happy and see your beautiful smile.

I was really very happy when I was with you—Maybe you will not believe me, maybe you think I have girls everywhere I go, but I want you to believe you are very special to me, you are so nice and caring, I wish I could stay with you all the time.

The future will tell us if this is possible, but even if I am not a very true follower of God, I will pray for us to be together very soon—I know I will go back to Bangkok next year, but I pray to come back this year.

I am not the best man on earth, but then, if I had been a very good man, I would not have met you! So I am very happy to know you and I hope you will wait for me and I hope that you have enough power to carry on.

I remember in your letter you wrote to me you have to try to carry on for your future and that you can reach up only suffering and you pray and you wish you could see a brighter day someday in the future—I hope I can help and bring some light to make each day a little brighter without suffering—Life is not easy, but I don't need to tell you, you know it better than me.

But I believe life is nice and I hope I can show you how nice it is, but you have to be strong and patient and you have to put your belief in yourself.

I think you are a very clever and intelligent girl, I hope you are also wise—You only need more knowledge, but this is the easiest thing to get.

Intelligence is given by birth, like beauty.

Knowledge is only information, like a fruit you only need to pick it up—But only intelligent people know how to use knowledge—I have met many stupid people who knew a lot but could not use it—You are a very beautiful and intelligent young girl who never had a chance to pick up the fruit—I hope you will have the time to start picking up the fruit soon.

Wisdom is something you get when mixing experience and intelligence and it is the most useful thing to have as it gives your brain and your heart the power to overcome and understand all situation.

If you are wise, you will have the power to wait for me and you will do an extra effort to learn some English.

I will show you how to make tomorrow brighter as soon as I can, but it is much easier if we can communicate directly and talk.

I typed this letter so that whomever has to translate can read it easier.

I LOVE YOU VERY VERY VERY MUCH AND CARE MORE ABOUT YOU THAN ABOUT ANY OTHER GIRL— TAKE CARE OF YOURSELF UNTIL I CAN TAKE CARE OF YOU.

LOVE.

Don't forget me, I'll always be there.

Love & Kisses.

દ્રૈ દ્રૈ દ્રૈ

Darling,

I am safely back in England. My address is on the back of this letter. Please write to me. I am sorry it has taken a long time for me to write to you.

I hope you can understand my writing and my English. Why don't you study English? It will be good for you.

I have bought a motorcycle for £225 and am working hard. The money is O.K., but I want more money. I want to be a very rich man. This year I think I will start my own business. When I am rich I will buy you a helicopter and B.M.W. car.

Darling, when we stayed together I loved you—but I don't know if you love me. Many times I think you only want me for my money. I remember you say to me 100 times "Buy me television." Even when you came with me to the airport you said to me many times "give me money."

દ્રૈ દ્રૈ દ્રૈ

Darling,

I'm in receipt of your letter which just arrived

The girl you met when you came to see me at NANA Hotel, I didn't know that he/she were an hermaphrodite and when somebody told me about I decided not to see her again.

I went twice to your place but unfortunately you were travelling to your father's home.

When you write that you came at <u>Gent</u> Hotel, it was at <u>Grace</u> Hotel I went when I returned after NANA'S.

I was so disappointed not to see you.

I have kept a so nice "souvenir" of my first stay in Thailand, when we went to the "Disco."

Please answer me as soon as you receive my letter, I might come to Bangkok very soon, I will let you know when.

Darling, I miss you, I do hope that you will continue to write me, telling what you are doing.

Are you still at school, are you working, how many boys friends have you got?

Many kisses from your lover.

≈ ≈ ≈

Darling,

I'm writing this at work on my Word Processor. This is just a short note to make sure you got my last letter— my brother wrote to you and I gave you £10. Hope it reach you O.K.

Whatever you do—Keep writing!! Every week. You know it makes me really happy when I read your letters and it lets me know that you are well and O.K. and not dead!!!

You know darling I really do miss you very much and am lonely without you. I miss Thailand and silly little things like you and me eating food together and sharing Khow Phat Moo or Pat Prio Wan, or going swimming together or riding in Tuk Tuk ("Fuck off Tuk Tuk"), and you hitting me.

I'm working hard now in London and hopefully should get a lot of work. When I work I get paid £7 an hour (about 300 baht).

Its really nice to know there's someone out there in the world who really cares for me—London is big, big, city—no one has any time for anyone else, nobody cares for anyone else. Yes, many Farang girl but I do not like any as much as my little Thai girl.

Please be careful and look after your body. STOP SMOKING & DRINKING & GET OUT Patpong. Why do you care for me darling—I'm just another horrible Farang! I'm glad you do.

Anyway keep writing those letters all me the time.

I <u>LOVE</u> you. Look after yourself my darling. In a few days I will send you my photos of family. My young brother says he wants to send you some good pictures of himself—May Law!!

Tell your girl friend take care of her body.

All my love.

Cuddlee Wuddlee.

❧ ❧ ❧

Darling,

You didn't cry too long after we said goodbye—you said you were not going to cry—"Taleh!"

In fact I was trying very very hard to keep my tears back, and after you left I was crying a little bit in the Airport.

I am really missing you darling, and thinking of you all the time—but I think one day you will take off with me from Don Muang Airport, I think you'll enjoy flying.

My family all like the photos of Thailand and all think you're very beautiful.

The only ones I didn't show them were the ones at Pattaya (mind you, I showed my brother) with you sitting on my head on the beach, and on my Kuay on the bed!

ès ès ès

Darling,

Thank-you for your letter which I got today. It made me smile very much, since I left Bangkok I have been very sad, I do not like England very much. The people here are very unfriendly, I prefer Thai people.

Also my work is not good at the moment. I have 2 bosses, but they have fallen out and do not speak to each other. Now the company I work for is changing very much and it is no fun. But soon I think it will be OK. I hope so.

Darling I think about you every day, it makes me happy to look at your photograph and think about you, but it also makes me unhappy because you are in Bangkok and I am in England. I wish we could be together again for even a short time. I hope you are in good health and everything is good for you.

I am fine but I do get depressed when I think of Thailand, I wish so much I could come back. But you know I have to work to earn more money.

Please be patient with me, for money. I promise to send you all the money you need direct to your bank, but right now it is difficult, because I have many debts to pay off first. But I will send you some money soon, in maybe 2 or 3 weeks. I will send as much as I can afford and then I will send you some more later. In England everything is very expensive and money does not last very long. Please wait a bit longer and I will send money.

I read again and again, the words you write in your letter to me, darling you know, you are very special to me also. You must believe me.

I learnt many good things from you, perhaps you don't understand this, but I saw things and felt things so good it made me change. Before I would lose my temper and get angry, but to spend time with you made me look at things differently.

Now perhaps I am more like Buddhist and I am a much better person.

Darling I hope you can understand all the words I write to you, they come from my heart.

ঞ ঞ ঞ

darling,

it is not good what happened.

tomorrow, not monday, i will leave, the ticket changed.

i like you, and i wish i could talk with you more.

you do not understand that i need my concentration and my heart for my work, my writing now.

many times i go out at night to be among people. not because i make love with many girls. i am not a butterfly.

i need to be among people to get new ideas and have time to think, and to relax from my writing.

i do not have other ladies.

and no lady goes to my apartment.

it is my place which i need for myself. i am not thai person.

you want too much now.

you destroy the concentration for my writing and i cannot write.

but this is important now for me.

you do not know a lot about western people.

people can be very different.

many things in thailand i do not like. i will not stay here forever.

i cannot get to know you without speaking, you cannot get to know me. i know it is difficult to learn english without school, but i cannot give you money now. i do not have.

i feel depressed many times and unhappy. this is bad, but also good for my writing.

i know it look strange how i behave.

if you want to be together with me please respect that i need time and inner space for myself now.

i not forget you.

i can be jealous too, and i would be sad to know you go with other man. not because make love is bad, but it does damage to your soul.

i think you not stupid. i think i want to be with you, but now not possible. i have to wait, and you: that is fair.

use the time and try to learn english, at least try.

many times there are misunderstandings among people. they are sad. gestures and meaning of things are different in many countries. rules of respect are different. feelings are different. ideas are different.

after I finish my writing i want to give you my heart. now i need my heart for writing.

i go out at night because for me it is hot at daytime. i come from a cold country.

many years in a very different country form people.

ε❧ ε❧ ε❧

Hello,

I'm 31, 6 foot, have my own business and Porshe and home and am now looking to settle down with the right woman of my choice. I'm told I'm good looking, a great lover, work too much and enjoy the finer things in life, plus basically work too hard. Since I got back to New Zealand I have gone out with several English, German and local women but find they're extremely finance orientated, selfish, untrustworthy and basically not what I've been looking for.

I was in Thailand with the army until recently and found the women most appealing, beautiful and faithful, just what I'm looking for.

Basically I am looking to marry a good looking woman who has a bit of class, can turn heads, and knows how to dress and handle herself socially. Someone who can take charge of the household accounts and deal with the staff in my absence. Someone prepared to eventually become involved in running my business, taking over if necessary.

Also a woman who can be trusted. Very important point in today's world where there seems so little trust. Be warned I am also looking for a woman to be the mother of my children and sexual partner. I find the woman here to be a little reserved sexually and find it difficult to accomodate my tastes and size. (I have an extremely large penis).

Bearing all I have said in mind and that I intend to be in Bangkok in the near future (as soon as business here is concluded). I would appreciate a brief and frank note from you as to what you seek in life, a brief history and several photographs (one preferably nude) so I can get an idea of what you're like! Alternatively a brief video.

Also please to provide details of education, parents, (family) and anything else you deem important. As I intend also to hopefully employ a Thai girl in the near future as my new house maid you might wish to see if any of your friends are possibly contemplating an overseas job in the near future.

As before I will require a brief history and photos for consideration. Hoping to hear from you shortly.

ॐ ॐ ॐ

(She is a good-looking, short, tough woman, 23, who sometimes appears as if she's on the verge of tears. Her painted, pointy fingernails torture a tiny piece of cellophane wrapper from her cigarette package as she speaks.)

I start work in Patpong four years ago. Flash Bar. I fall in love with farang, this second time. First time New Zealand man. He with me for one year. We break because he take me to school for learning haircut but he don't trust me. I don't know what he want. I don't know why he go back. He don't trust me for money. Don't trust me for school. He think I still work Patpong. Two years ago, New Zealand boy, he teach me how to be strong, how to be alone. He nice. Now I love Denmark for one year. Still in love together because he say, "You don't have to work in that stupid place." Sometime I bored, have to go to bar and that's why we fight, fight. Fight because sometimes he too jealous, too boring. I go out talk to girlfriend and I like to stay with girlfriend more than him. Denmark sometime boring. Sometime good.

(why did you start working as a bar girl?)

First time because I with Thai boyfriend and have one baby. I working 70 baht one day, work 12 hour, making belt, making earring, making lighter, making anything for a company in Bangkok. I come Patpong because I hear good money. I can make home better. I want to live better. We no have enough money. We stay together long time, we work together. I did not know how to take a pill to not get pregnant.

(why are there so many bar girls in Thailand?)

If Thai boyfriend is good and take care of girl, Thailand not be full of prostitutes. But they have baby and not take care, not get married. That's why they have prostitutes. Also, somebody not want marry girl second time if she not virgin. That's why they become prostitutes. I have a lot of friend do work like I did before. Thai boyfriend never take care their baby because he have to work hard, can't find the money to take care of baby. It's a problem of money also.

(do bar girls make good money?)

If don't take smack, don't take a drink, don't have Thai boyfriend to look after.

(why did you attempt suicide?)

Want to show, when boyfriend shouting, want boyfriend say, "Sorry." I try two times. With knife, and one time with scissor. First time two and a half years ago because I have problem with my boyfriend. We go out to Patpong, have a drink. Some people talk to me. I like to talk with somebody else. So we fight. Just jealous. Sometime another boyfriend call me for his girlfriend, so he don't trust. Stupid thing. I do silly. Sometime I learn English, I come home late.

I try to kill me second time, last year, because my boyfriend he go back Europe for nearly four months. Tell me about the place he living no telephone number. One day, I drunk in Patpong. I want to talk to him. I feel lonely. I just wait thinking how I feel. I miss him. Have no telephone number. I call his mother to get his number. Then I call his apartment. A woman answer. She ask, say, "Who are you?" I told the farang girl, "Ask the boy, he know very well." Boyfriend say how I know this telephone number? I say his mother give to me. He say he call me back tomorrow. I say, "Why you not talk with me now? Because you have lady? Tell me the truth." Next day he call me. We fight. Before, he told me he come back now. On telephone, he tell me one and a half month more. Say he not finish work. I say, "What happen about lady?" He told me the story what happen. Lady from Denmark have no find a place to live, sleep on his floor. I think 50 percent I do believe, 40 percent no believe. I thinking I lonely. Not have man four months. Woman same like man. I go Koh Samui. Meet man. Nice. Denmark come back. We fight. I tell him, I love him but I feel lonely, that why I do this. So he don't talk with me, don't kiss me, don't look at me for nearly one week. I cut my arm because he don't trust me. I try to kill me because nobody trust me.

(will you try to kill yourself again?)

I don't think so because I thinking about my daughter. If I die, who take care of her? She four year and a half.

(what is your future?)

Now have two boyfriends. Denmark man never say he want take care of me forever. Australia man say he want take care of me forever. Australia man worried about my daughter also. I don't love the friend of Australia. Just friend. I do love Denmark man.

(why do some girls take drugs?)

I tell you the truth? Because people want good sex. Because the tourists like. They have money. Say, "Come on, we have good fun together." The girl don't know what this is. I drink and smoke ganja because we go to discotheque to meet some people.

(what is your advice to a new girl thinking about becoming a bar girl?)

A lot girl from north Thailand finish with Thai boyfriend, have broken heart, ask me, "What about farang boyfriend? How can have? I want have same as you, go another country. Have gold, have house, have good money in the bank, have nice dress, buy things for parents." She see some friend who have more than her. She say, "Why? What her story?" I tell, "Please forget about this. It's not fun. Now AIDS coming in Thailand. People look down at bar lady. Some people go work first time, get lucky, meet man, take care this girl. But maybe you don't find man take care you. You have to sleep around. Sometimes man look like shit, have to fuck him."

(do you know any bar girls who married foreigners?)

Eleven of my friend in the same bar stop work and marry with farangs. Netherland, England, German, Denmark also.

(when you go with a customer you don't like, what do you think about while making love?)

Thinking about how to be strong. What tomorrow to pay. What tomorrow to eat. Want some money to send back to parents.

(do your parents know what work you do?)

My mother she know. My father he don't know because he never ask. I bring two boyfriend to my parents already. I told my mother. Because I send money to her, she ask me, "How do you find the money?" I say the truth. She say, "If you do like this, you not thinking about your future." She say, "Take care of yourself, don't go about take drugs." She say, "Come stay home, better." The first boyfriend, my mother don't like. New Zealand. She like Denmark. He helped make the kitchen, cleaning, take water from the river. He good looking, nice, polite, quiet.

(why do so many Western men like Thai bar girls?)

They like the brown skin and black hair. A lot of farang women, after get married, get fat. Thai women different from farang. Europe women are prostitutes only to take drugs. Thai women are prostitutes to take care their families.

(what is it like having a foreign boyfriend who lives in another country?)

Sometimes it boring waiting waiting for these guys. We don't know when they come back. Or if they change. And then we lose the time. I hate when people leave, when my boyfriend go back. I like to talk with old people, from England, because I hear good story, something I never hear before.

(how will you decide which of your two boyfriends to stay with?)

I have to wait. Now I play a game, two games, with two boyfriends. Some people have to show me they love me and my daughter also.

🐤 🐤 🐤

Darling,

How's life going with you now? Hope you continue with hair dressing course and come over here to work in Australia and New Zealand to start a business.

I know your life has been not that good working at those clubs, but you have a chance to do good things and perhaps find a European man to marry you and give you comfort & love which is lasting and not short time.

Give it a try darling, there's men out there who don't want short-time love and want life-time love with beautiful Asian women who'll be honest to them. That's what Floyd wants, a wife and children from Asia. You are beautiful lady darling, use it to do good things.

If you like I could find you someone to marry and bring you over here. You'd like it here. It's up to you.

Please write back to me, I think you are still good darling, please be honest to me and keep in touch. We'll see each other soon.

ð ð ð

My dear little Monkey!

How are you? I'm fine. I'm writing you for two reasons. The first is because I like you and I want to keep in touch so I can meet you again, next time I will come to Thailand, but only if you want as well of course. The other reason is that I owe you 300 baht. I'm very sorry that I didn't come to see you (and pay you before I left), but when I came to my room, my friend was there and he had been stabbed with a knife in his back, by a Thai girl on Sukhumvit Road. He had a lot of pain and was very dizzy because he had taken a lot of pain killers and he had fever. I will send you the money, I promise, but if you want, it's up to you. Because I'm not sure this is the right address. You didn't give it to me, maybe you don't want to see me again. Ha! Ha! So if you write me and tell me that you received this letter and give me the address, I will send you the money in my next letter to you.

I know you think I am a big butterfly, and that's true, maybe I am the biggest butterfly you met, but I can't help it. But still it's something special with you. I like you very much even if I think you can be very miserable sometimes. But, butterfly or not you are the same as me, the only difference with us is that I pay and you get paid. I know you think I am a bit crazy, perhaps it's true, but that's the way I am. Hope to hear from you soon, I promise again to send you the money but first you have to answer this letter, fair enough? Promise me to take care and don't go home with some fucking idiot who hits you or something like that. Send my regards to your sister if you see her. Be careful, many kisses from me. Love.

$\approx$ $\approx$ $\approx$

Darling,

I would like to be in Bangkok but I am in France. This is BIG problem without solution for the moment.....

I work now again in my nursery between trees and orchids. I dream and work. Is better to work and also to dream.

I think very often at what you spoke me in the tuk tuk one night in your area. "Tomorrow is finish." I don't arrive to imagine if you spoke seriously or if it was just to be tranquil and sniff your cotton?

I would like only one thing now. Go back in Thailand and this desire is not ready to disappear rapidly.

This is my dream: Take a fly today and see you tomorrow.

Darling is like a dream and I like this dream.

Try the music of Johnny Clegg. He was Number one in France in 87 and I never listen in Bangkok.

ॐ ॐ ॐ

Darling,

How are you?

Since I leave Bangkok, I write to you some letter but you never answer!!! Anyway, I hope you receive this one. And you try to answer to me. The hazard don't exist if I meet you. It was because I have to meet you. You are mole of the weather, the blue sky, the rainbow. You are the one who open my eye. I know now—I know now who you are.

See you soon!

Don't forget!

See you soon!

PS: Send me a photograph of you—if you want. Thank you.

ॐ ॐ ॐ

Hallo, my Thai girl! How are you?

I cannot say how much I'm happy about all letters from you. Now, I know how beautiful love you have and you give me so much lovely feeling to my heart. You touch my heart so soft and deep, I cannot say how much satisfaction you give to my soul. Now, I know why I love you so much, sure never before I have feeled so much love in my life and never before I have had a exciting girlfriend like you my darling.

Oh my darling what can I give back to you, I don't have. I cannot feel so deep in my heart and I don't have so beautiful love like you. Oh yes my darling, I'm so happy to have a great love like you. I wish I can write so to you darling but you know I cannot because you don't give me. I can write about my heart, I can write about my soul, but I think it's not important for you to hear. I think, you don't like to stay in a love story with a man. I tried to phone to you several time. On your birthday in the morning, I waited fifteen minutes but I did not talk to my love and two day ago I waited fifteen minutes again and any Thai girl told to me, darling is working. I thought, oh my God working, I thought fucking in Bangkok and I feeled so much bad that I was crying for my beautiful love.

Darling, my head told to me, no problem for you it's more easy for you to make fuck than to learn A.B.C.D. in English. Darling, my head told me it's more easy to make fuck in Bangkok than to write letters to me. Darling my heart is crying to hear this. Tell me what can I do?

I don't know that my money arrived your bank. I don't know what do you think about my letters? I don't know do you have love, have you? But I know, you fuck for money, I think it's really boring and dirty. I think you cannot give any satisfaction to your soul when you make fuck but I'm not sure maybe you can. Please tell me I want to know, I want to have answer for this question. But, maybe you don't know and I want that you think about this question every time when you are fucking with a man and I want that you think to me, too.

My soul is suffering that I know that you make fuck. I know, you are only strong with the mouth but your head you cannot use because you are too lazy to learn this. You know for fuck you don't need your head but anytime you must learn to use your head, my love. Oh yes I know, you are sleeping girl because everytime when we stayed together I said you look in my eyes but you cannot.

For this kind of people I say sleeping people and never I spent time with this people. Do you remember to Koh Samui, I bought a ticket to Bangkok for you because people like you cannot give love but my heart told me you can try to wake up darling. I think soon I come to Bangkok for holiday maybe you like to see me again but no problem if you don't like, I can stay alone in Thailand and I can look around without you. I think this is the last time that I talk about my great feeling in my life when I try to love a girl. This is the last time to ask you for love if you don't answer. I think you are on the right way to stop me. I want to say all my love to you but you can not feel all my love.

Bye-bye my sleeping love and have a good time in Bangkok.

❧ ❧ ❧

Sweetest lady,

Why aren't we together?

Every little practical problem gets so complicated because we live thousands miles apart from each other!

I had to devote so many hours today to this very trivial money problem between my bank and yours! After several phone calls, my bank told me that the money I sent you has definitely be transferred to the Bangkok Bank Ltd. Thailand.

It seems there is a problem somewhere between the central Bangkok Bank office and the Branch which manages your account. Tonight, I shall go to the Post Office and send you a facsimile of the transfer document.

Then you can show this document to your bank and claim that the money must be credited to your account, because this money is definitely and officially in possession of the Bangkok Bank, while its legal owner is you and nobody else!

I truly hope this matter will be solved by the time you receive this letter, because I do not wish that such down-to-earth problems can get between us and make our lives more difficult than it already is.

I cannot express how much I <u>hate</u> money! Why does money have to come between people when the only important things are love and the will to be happy together?

I have been dreaming of you last night after your phone call. It was the most delightful dream possible: there was a big party going on where all my French friends meet you for the first time. Everybody was very happy and everything was nice and smooth...Then I woke up, and it was a rather cold and rainy day in France.

It was only a dream, but I am sure it will come true some day, and that this huge party with all my friends gathering together to meet you here will actually take place shortly.

I had dinner with my friends on Tuesday. We have been talking about you, and they asked me to send you their respects.

My loveliest lady, I hope I will get a letter from you very soon, which will enlighten my day. I love you more than words can tell and I am anxiously looking forward to the day we shall meet again.

I'm currently taking care of this problem of money transfer between France and Thailand. Be sure I will never let you down.

Take very good care of yourself and please do not forget this farang, very far from Thailand, who loves you and thinks of you every second of his life.

Tons of love.

🐢 🐢 🐢

Darling,

This is in reply to your Advertisement in the Trade & Exchange.

Will start by telling you a little about myself, I am 39 years of age 5' 11" in height of muscular build and 13 1/2 stone.

I have my own Business here in New Zealand, there always seems to be plenty of work, I find myself working 7 days most weeks.

I have many interests, which include fishing, tramping, reading, music, travel, etc. I collect paintings and spoons.

I had planned to visit Thailand recently, then thought it best to wait until I could have a friend that I could visit and who could show me about. I did advertise in one of the Bangkok papers but only got one reply from a guy who is gay. I'm easy going and very open-minded, but must admit I'm not into male gays.

I'm looking forward to visiting Thailand as I've always found your country very fascinating.

I would be happy to hear from you darling, and hope we can develop a lasting friendship.

Until then.

Kindest Regards.

🐢 🐢 🐢

Darling,

I hope you can read my writing. Sorry I cannot write in Thai.

I hope my letter arrives at your place. It is five days since I said goodbye to you. I remember very clearly our time together. I worry for you very much. Please be very careful of any sickness. I love you and want you to live happily for a long time. I think of you everyday, but at night time I want to cry when I think of you at your job. Please only be with a good man. I wish it was me. I feel love for you and will never forget you. Be my darling and try to think of me and remember me. I'd love to be with you now. I feel in love with you. You are so beautiful. So sweet and soft. Don't be sad with yourself. Look ahead and find a good future. Study English and put hope in Buddha. Always try hard.

Do you play my song "Stay" by Jackson Brown? I remember singing it to you. That song will always remind me of you and your beautiful long hair, dark eyes and smooth skin. You're so beautiful and so sweet to me. My darling, please write to me using the envelope I've included. Also please confirm your bank number. I will send some money to help you as much as I can. Leave some space in your heart for me. I think of you always.

P.S. Can you send me your photo? I need to see.

≈ ≈ ≈

(Plain looking, small and quiet, she is 23, a little nervous about being interviewed but is willing to answer some questions.)

I work Patpong five years. Work no good. I don't like this work because I'm Thai lady and I think it's no good for lady to meet too many man. Before, I love, but he have another girlfriend farang. He from Belgium. Today not love. Now we be friend.

64

(do you believe the love letters you receive from other men?)

No. 20 percent, I think true. Some lie, some true. I feel I know. We talk together in Bangkok. But in the letter, different talk. When we talk in Bangkok is different. Letter is higher, more, more. This is not true.

(what sort of future do you want?)

I not think about future. Life OK now. Little bit problem. Some man fun, some not. Some man so nice, he want to be happy. Want me to give happy. Man is 50-50 fun. I happy when I see him from Belgium. Only looking, talk, no more. I know he cannot give me more. I don't like farang he look me down. I think everybody same. Not only farang, also Thai look me down sometime. Some. Farang come look, "Eeeeeeeeeeeeeeeeeeee! Very bad girl!" Crazy thing. Some farang crazy. If we speak true, they don't believe. If we speak lie, they believe.

(what truths don't they believe?)

Like lady work inside bar, because my work, have every day check, we have clinic, we check AIDS. I know one man, England, he say, "Why you too expensive? Another girl 100 baht." I say, "OK, you go 100 baht. Maybe she give you something, AIDS. What she can give you?" I tell him, "Me? 2,000 baht. For 100 baht you cannot buy clinic. You cannot buy medicine. You can only buy taxi." I scared AIDS. Use condom. Sometimes man say, "I don't want." I say, "If don't want, I cannot do." He say, "OK." But sometime he crazy and take off. If lady don't see, he take off. I say, "No. Cannot do."

65

(do the bar girls lie in letters to their customers?)

I know they speak (she imitates a high-pitched, sing-song voice), "How are you? I love you! Take care yourself! Don't work too much!" Me, I tell 80 per cent true because I don't like to speak lie. I speak, "love," but not true. I never love! (laughs). I lie. I don't want hurt somebody. But if I not say love, maybe he not think nothing.

(do you know many bar girls who have married foreign men?)

I know three my friends marry farang. My good friend she come visit Thailand, they happy. He take care everything. He from Hawaii. They stay Hawaii.

(what problems do you have with customers?)

Crazy man want to hurt me. Sadist. I say, "Don't do." Swiss. He ask me what I like. I say, "I don't like hurt." He be nice to me. He good man. He understand. He told me, "Lady from Europe like a man hurt she." I don't know, but I see in a photo, he don't know I see in his open locker. Wow! Picture he do with lady. He make lady hurt sex. Photo him hurt her with belt and tie her hands down. I see in his room the long whip. Another my friend lady go with Korea man. He tell lady, cut her arm. He want look. He happy see blood. He Korea.

❧ ❧ ❧

Darling,

Now I must give you an honest explanation of why I could not let you come to my room (last night in Bangkok). This is the honest truth, darling.

When you came to see me and kissed me goodbye I thought you were saying goodbye forever and that you wanted to finish with me. I began to cry because I felt very, very bad. You know I want to see you very, very much. I felt so lonely. I wanted to talk with someone. I felt very weak and very, very sad. The only person I could talk to was that other girl. You had gone and I thought you were not going to come back. So I telephoned the other girl and she offered to come to my room and talk to me and comfort me. She knows I love you. She slept on my bed but I did <u>not</u> make love to her. She is a friend but not my lover.

When you came back to my room, she was in my room and I did not want you to know. I was very afraid you would think I was a butterfly. So I could not let you in and make you even more angry. So I said to you I would write to you and come back to Thailand to see you. I am very, very sorry, darling, because I wanted you to be with me that night. She left my room soon after you came and I went back to Australia very lonely and very sad.

I am to blame, darling, not you. It is not your fault. I should apologise to you and I say to you I am very, very sorry.

Please forgive me.

Please enjoy using the things I gave you. Please do not throw them away. Ask your sister to make you a shirt from the cotton I gave you. I think it will look lovely on you.

<u>COMING BACK TO SEE YOU</u>

I have already made a reservation to come back to Bangkok, <u>to see you</u>, soon. Please come to meet me at the airport.

Please darling tell me what you think about me. Do you like my body, am I too old for you, do you like me? I want to know how you feel about me.

If you have decided you do not want me, please tell me.

≈ ≈ ≈

Hello Darling,

Two days ago I received your 2 letters (on the same day). Thank you very much, it made me very happy. I hope by now you have my letter I sent you. When I read your first letter I was shocked a little. You told me that police catch you at Malaysia Hotel (working but then I do not understand very well. Did you stay 3 days in <u>Prison or not</u>, and did you have to pay 5,000 baht <u>or not</u>. <u>Please tell me</u>.) Did you receive the money I sent you? Soon my friend will send you some money. I asked him before I left and I trust him, so he will surely send it.

Darling, about the police catching you at Malaysia Hotel. You know your kind of job. Many people from all over the world are coming to Thailand for that (you know). And I think that the police doesn't want it any more! Anyway you do what you like, but I ask you to be careful. I hope you will take my advice. I know you meet many man (By now, I don't know how many write letter to you!) But my hope is that you will not forget me. I surely will not forget you.

About me, I am fine. I work here in Cambodia already 6 weeks and in 4 1/2 month I will finish. Everyday I see many wounded man from the war, and it is not a pleasant sight. But when I go home I will stop 1 or 2 weeks in Thailand so I can see how your visa is going on. And I hope you can come to Belgium.

Darling, do you still have your little rabbit? You bought it just before I left. And I was angry (do you remember). I know, I was many times angry but that was because I care for you <u>too</u> much.

Do you still share room with your friend or not? Is your mother still in Bangkok? When she is, give her my greetings.

Also give my greetings to everyone who lives together with you. Also did your friend get the photos I sended her? I hope she has and that she was happy with the photos.

So darling this is all for now. Don't forget that I wait for your letters. It is the only thing I have here. When you work, be careful and remember all the things I told you. I worry a lot about you. Please sign the letters you send yourself, you know I like that. And may God bless you, your family and your friends.

🐸 🐸 🐸

Hello, my great love!

How are you?

I don't know what I can write to you my lovely darling because it's sorrowful so much I feel that I cannot stay with you, now. So beautiful-looking and happiness smile on the pictures what you sent to me I have not seen when I stayed with you. Yes of course I jealous of all men who can stay with, now. Sure before I know you I did not have any problems in my life but now I have because I love you so much. I cannot stay with a girl here in Germany because my heart wants to wait for you only.

Sure, darling I want to stay with you all time in my life and never I want to stop you again but now I must stop to listen to my heart so much, I have to start to listen to my head again. My head tell to me, be careful of this girl maybe you only look for money every time and you think I love you so much and I send money enough to solve the problems of your family. I'm so sorry for you my great love but I have never seen your love in Thailand only show of love and I'm still not married with you and so I cannot help to solve the problems. I think, you will forever have problems with money to your family because your father drink too much and he cannot make enough money for your mother. Sure, darling my great love if we are married I want to give some money to your mother but now I cannot help you and I hope you will understand me, my darling. I want that you know, I'm not in my life to look for money! I stay in life to look for love *only*. I know, I need money too. But if I need money I have and sure if you really like to stay with me forever and for love, I will have money for you too. Every time I want to look for you and I want try to make you happy so much but don't forget every time I look for love only. I don't know why, but I think you have great love and maybe you really want to give me, you can be sure I'm happy so much and every time I want try to give back to you. But now, I feel bad and I wish you stay here with me, my great love.

Please, write more letters to me..... please don't let me wait so much time for one letter more. I need more confirmation of your love to me. I want try to believe, that you will make a Passport and I don't want that you make fuck for a Passport and so I want send some money to your Bank. But now I don't have any time to go to the Bank. I think in the next week I will take some time to send some money to you for a *Passport*. My great love I have to stop to write to you because it's too late now and I must sleep. I want to say thank you so much for the nice pictures and for the beautiful letter. My great love, I want to hear that you want to marry me in Bangkok. I hope! I can believe your love to me because without love it's not possible to have a great time together.

I only can say to you, STOP to make fuck for money because we have too much AIDS on this world now.

I don't want to see you die, I want to love you a long time.

All my love to you.

I'm missing you.... I'm missing you..... missing you..... missing.....

tell me how much money?

§ § §

(She's pretty, 21, with silver bracelets, lots of rings and a blue-striped, white shirt tucked into beat-up gray shorts.)

I work one-and-half year Patpong, in Pink Panther and Pussy Connection. I like work, dancing, and have bikini. I don't like work dancing no bikini. I shy. People looking sometime no good. Many look pussy. Before, I go in Sweden. I stay Sweden only one month. I want to stay more. Cannot. In Sweden I make Thai food, clean room, iron clothes. Sometimes see TV. I don't understand, little bit I understand. Outside, walking, looking, maybe 30 minutes and come back in the room.

(what is your work in Patpong Road like?)

Sometimes good, sometimes no good. Sometimes for fun. Sometimes for love. I stay with same man one month. I love him. I never forget him. He come back, he forget me. What can I do? Maybe 10 people write me letters. Only one man from Norway help me, every month send money. I don't believe other letters. Bullshit. Everywhere people write, love me, want see me again. I never see

71

money in the bank for me. They only say, "Love, love, love, love, love." I don't think so. Everywhere farang say, "Love Thai lady. Beautiful, beautiful." Bullshit. Sometime I write, "I don't want working Patpong. I want you send money for me in the bank. I wait you come back." I write, "I'm happy with you." Sometimes I tell I love man. Sometimes farang say, "You want go with me?" I say, "How much you give me?" He say, "How much you want?" I say, "2,000 baht, 1,500 baht." Sometimes I like only one man, I want to stay with him for free. Sometimes not for love, I cannot stay alone. In the bar, one month, I get maybe 3,000 to 4,000 baht. If I work other job, shop, I get maybe 800 baht. In bar, I sometimes work only two days, Monday and Friday. Sometimes no money. Farang say, "Go for free." I say, "Fuck off! I don't want go for free."

(why do men write you letters?)

I don't know why they write letters. Sometimes bullshit. Sometimes I write letter to man and he not write me back. I think he write for fun. He write for sex. Some girls think bullshit letters. Some girls think he like the girl. Sometimes lady believe him. I think farang come Thailand for holiday, for fucking. I think he like lady Thai because beautiful, take care him and good love, good heart. I don't think lady farang same. Lady farang not take care of him and think about herself. Or she butterfly.

(are there any differences in the nationalities of your customers?)

I don't like Japan. Like sadist. Hit me very hard and bite me. No fun. Bite me like a dog. I think he Japan. Sadist. Other man, Europe, nice, take shower with me.

(what would be your advice to a young girl who is considering being a bar girl?)

I say, up to her. She want to work, she work. First time I work in Patpong bar as bartender. I was 19. I had Thai boyfriend and one baby with him. Baby come, I go Patpong work as bartender two month. Then pussy bar, dancing. First time I go with farang I don't know where he come from. First time I scared. I think maybe no good. I think only money. Money for baby. I think 1,000 baht. After, I think, good. Only short time.

(how has your life changed after working with foreigners?)

I cannot speak English before. Only say, "Thank you," "Give me money," "I hungry," and "I go home." Now I can speak Sweden, German, French, Italy, English, only little bit. Sometimes I happy. Sometimes good. I love him only from Norway. He go Philippines. I think he stay Singapore now. After he go Norway, send me money. I know him only two months. Good money pay for me. I want shirt, he buy shirt. I want jean, he buy jean. I want camera, he buy camera. And tape cassette, big, he buy for me and give me 6,000 baht and go Philippines. He say, "I want you finish working fucking farang. I want stay with you and baby." Baby one-year-eight-months. And he send money to me in the bank. Now I wait him. Him say he go back and send me money, 10,000 baht, and next year he come back and want to take me Norway. I want to know some people like me and not only for fucking and fun. I want somebody hold me, and I think he like me sometime. He say, "I like you." Never say love you. And I say, "I like you." Never say love you.

(were you ever in love with a foreigner before?)

Only one time. Broken heart. From England. First him like me. I like him too. I stay with him one month. I go Patpong work again. I saw he took my friend for fucking. Now he get married my girlfriend.

(what do you think is the difference between Thai women and foreign women?)

Thai lady and farang lady not same. I think farang lady hate Thai lady. Norway he told me he have farang lady. He go work two months, three months, come back, girlfriend fucking brother he. Lady farang look down Thai lady very bad. Why they look me like that? Maybe jealous. Because many farang boy come and only stay Thai lady, not with farang lady.

(what do your parents do?)

My mother, father sell food, chicken, eggs and vegetable. Mother, father not angry me. No problem. Sometimes I give money. Now they not working. Every month, I give maybe 2,000 baht, maybe 1,000 baht. If I don't have money I think too much.

(do you worry about AIDS?)

I'm scared, you know, AIDS. I take condom every day. I say, "No condom, I don't want fucking with you, I go home. If you take condom, I fucking with you." Before, with Sweden man boyfriend, I don't take condom. I scared.

≈ ≈ ≈

My Darling,

I will do only that way, which makes you happy. When you think you live happier in Thailand, then I'm very sad, but I will say OK. When you mean, you are happier in Germany, then you are in every time welcome as my wife.

You know that my love to you is without an end. You are more for me than a normal wife. You are my wife, my little spoiled daughter and the mother of our baby, although we were stupid to give away our good baby.

I feel that your way of life is to go off of me. When this way makes you happy, then it's well for you. But perhaps you will be unhappy in the way without me. That would be a pity for you and for me.

Soon there will be the last time I shall come to Thailand for you. Last time I paid a lot of money and came for nothing to Thailand. I think that soon we shall have the last chance to find together. For me I can repeat always the same about you: I love you more than every other lady and I miss you every day and night.

When you would like to go off of me, I shall also miss your family. I like your mother and father. I like your three sisters and your two brothers. I thought always that they are my family too.

Naturally you are the most important person of your family.

Last year was very important for me. I thought that at this day it was our marriage with your and my family and the most important, it was the marriage of us in front of your and my God. When you and me were bound with the line, I thought now we are bound for our whole life.

But darling, you can believe me, I'm not angry about you, I wish only that you are happy.

In the last time I think very often to the time one year ago with you. You remember we made together something for the Christmas time. For me it was a happy time, because I hoped that you will have our baby in your body. I thought always, when you have a baby of me, you will never go off of me. Our baby I loved very, very much. But perhaps I'm only stupid.

❧ ❧ ❧

Hello my dear!

How are you, I hope fine! I go to work since three weeks.

In my work I always be at home at the weekend. If you want to phone me always on a Sunday. When I worked, my wife caught your letter, but you know that I leave my wife. I think that we meet again, because I love you. I am searching for a new apartment, if you want come to me, to Germany. Please looking for your passport and all what you need to leave your country. If you want come to me send me your complete name and your address and I will send you a ticket.

As I have a apartment you should come. (Maybe a half-past or shorter).

If I leave my wife I have to pay for three children. The money then is shorter for us but we can get it on together!!

If you don't come I only can visit you at January. I miss you really and I wish me that you come. I hope you get my first letter, I was in a bad time with myself. My friend write for me this letter in English. I hope you can translate my first letter. I cannot write every letter in English because my friend lives a long way from here.

❧ ❧ ❧

Dear Lovely Darling!

How are you "darling?"

At first I must say sorry to you. Because I didn't write a letter more fast.

Do you know what I am, busy in my job. I remember that you said, "You must take time to yourself." And I agree with you. When I back to Japan, I want to do so, I did try make time to me. But I could not take a time until now.

Didn't you think that while I forget you. I never forget you, your exotic lovely smile, and your kind mind.

I want meet you soon. I want hold you soon.

Last time I told you that I shall back to Thailand soon. But now I can tell you that I will back on next month. Maybe I stand on Bangkok very soon. That time, I can take 4 days holiday with you. Please give me time that I can stay with you.

Then I have trip to Hong Kong, Kuala Lumpur and Thailand. After Thailand, I go to Manila and Taipei.

Will you please give me a letter. I wait your letter.

Before I call on Bangkok, I will give you telephone.

So then I bring some picture that is yours. And go to trip to somewhere on Thailand with together.

Next I will send a post card which is taken by me at Thailand.

Thank you. GOOD BYE!

P.S. Now I am studying Thai. I want talk with you more, I want to know you more deep! See you!!

Don't be care. I promise to go to your side soon.

My Lovely Darling, I don't forget my promise which I buy KIMONO or YUKATA for you. But now is winter in Japan. So that I can't find YUKATA. Please wait until summer season.

Thank you. I hope, want to get your next letter with kind from Bangkok.

THANKS AND GOOD BYE.

🐌 🐌 🐌

(She has sharp features, thin lips and a triangular face framed by silver hoop earrings. She laughs easily and frequently, and sometimes bugs out her eyes for emphasis.)

I am 31. I three years working. Farang so different than Thai man. When stay together, I think it's good. Farang man make love better! Yeah! (laughs) I have boyfriend now, Danish man, really fucking good! (laughs) I love him. With Thai man, when he lie down, he just come. Never make me feel romantic. I know Danish man two years. I love him because he very good here in heart and good in brain. I know him now. Always when he stay with me, he always make good for me, never jealous to me. Free style. And he tell me he love me. He have three girlfriends, Danish, and he tell me he don't want to bullshit. He not bullshit to me. He say to me, "I think I love Thai girl better. Danish girl always like this (she puts her nose up in the air). Very, very jealous." He hate that. He like the style of me. That's why he love me and (laughs) he fuck me very perfect! I can tell you this true. And he give me heart and feeling. I say to him, "You fuck perfect!" (laughs) That's why I love Europe man.

Before I work in the bar, I make cocktails. Not go-go. I work Love Boat Bar. I like, because I can mix cocktail. Very good cocktail. I meet him there with the cocktail. He sit and quiet and try to talk with me and miss me.

Not playboy. One week, he come everyday to Love Boat.

(how many men write letters to you?)

I don't remember. Some people funny, some people love me. I hear a lot some people love me. First guy from Switzerland. He finish make love, say, "Oooh, you so good. I like you, you're my style!" (laughs) After he stay with me long time, he say love me. A lot of man, it's bullshit. I don't believe the man. I never believe them. Even my Danish boyfriend. Because I had a broken heart with a Thai boyfriend.

(why did you start working as a bar girl?)

I have one baby. The father is Thai. I don't know who to take care of me, I have no boyfriend, my mom very old. I don't want this work.

(what was your first time as a bar girl with a foreigner?)

I'm scared. I remember, I never forget. Australian. First man. I know I want money. He say, "Don't be scared. I don't make love with you, I take you, I sleep you, that enough." We no make love.

(and the first time you made love with a foreign customer?)

I don't remember the country of the man. I feel scared. I say, "Oh, my god." He say, "Don't be scared. You want money? You have to be and enjoy. I make you feel good." I say, "OK." I take a shower. I come to bed. He hold me, say, "You scared?" I say, "A little." He kiss me. I feel better.

(what is your future?)

I think I marry Danish. He ask me. I say, "I want, but think you have to take time, look me long, long time. Maybe I good, maybe I bad."

(when you answer letters from customers, what do you write?)

I say, "Yeah, I hope so you come back very soon. How are you? You work so hard. Don't care about the work, if you like me you come back for me."

(do you write that you love them even if you don't?)

Sometime I make bullshit. I never ask money. Sometime I write, "I love you. I like you very much." It's bullshit.

(why do you write it then?)

Because I know this guy bullshit to me. He holiday, he playboy. I know he don't tell me the truth. He say, "I love you." I say, "I love you too." He can write what he want, I can write what I want. (laughs)

(how does Thai society react to you?)

No problem for me. I don't care because I know Thai man jealous Thai girl stay with farang. He don't like it. Because he don't know.

(why are Thai men jealous of farangs?)

He dress better. He have money.

(does your mother know about your work?)

My mother, she don't know. I say, "Work in shop, disco, make a cocktail." I don't want her to know. But I never tell her because no good for her have daughter like this because my mom don't want me to be like this. I think I want to tell her about Danish.

(why do some girls commit suicide or take hard drugs?)

Some girl maybe broke her heart. Because they take a tablet and get stoned, maybe think too much, "Oooh my life," why she have to do.

(are you ever sad enough to consider suicide?)

I never sad about this. I think I'm strong enough. I learn a lot about people, about love, because I broke heart before. What work I can do?

(what advice would you give a new girl who is thinking about becoming a bar girl?)

I say no good if she very young, 15 or 12. If 25, she can do what she want.

(what is the difference in men's nationalities?)

Japan I don't like. I don't know why. He sadist. When I work, only one, he a sadist with me. He give me 2,000 baht for one minute and I leave. He say, "Take off clothes." I take off. I put a towel cover my body. I have to stand up like this and he say, "Show me bikini underwear." And he do like this (she gestures, masturbating like a man). He hit me with the hands on my bottom. I get hurt. I say,

"Whoa," say, "Bye-bye." He give me money and say, "Bye-bye." Thai girls, my friends, they don't like Japanese men. They say sadist. I think I like Denmark. Number two, Oslo, Norway. Number three, Scandinavian also, Finland. I don't like American. I never get a boyfriend there. Not my style. Lot American want take me, but I say, "No, not my style." They always (she puts her nose in the air again). He think, oh, he handsome, very tall. That's why I don't like. German, I don't like. Talk very bad. Not very nice.

(do you make enough money?)

Money OK. I stay my own home. Two rooms, one toilet. Baby girl, three-and-half-years. I want to give her a good life, good school, good work. I think I can do. I don't want her to be like this. Very bad. I don't think it so good. I know. If I marry with my boyfriend, I change the country and bring her. I want her to have a good idea so she can make something good.

(does your Danish boyfriend know about your life?)

I tell him the truth. I tell him, "Before, work Patpong." He ask me many questions. My boyfriend send 20,000 baht me every month. One my girlfriend get money sent her every month from boyfriend Europe and she spend this money on her farang boyfriend here, drinks and eat and everything. And the man who send money don't know what she doing.

(what do the foreign men in the bars really want, sex or love?)

Some people holiday. Some people not. Some people work in Thailand and want girl long time. Some say,

"Want to stay with Thai girl all my life." Some take holiday, say, "I don't care about the girl, I want make love."

(what are you thinking about while you make love to a customer you don't really like?)

Not feel good. I not show my feeling. I think, "OK, I want make very soon and then go home." If some guy I don't like, OK make love, but I don't look his face. I don't kiss him. I don't like these people drunk.

(what sort of men go to Patpong?)

I think they lonely. That's why they come out every day. Nothing to do. Maybe he need a girl. Long time no fuck a girl. Sometime farang girl take Thai girl. Sometime with the wife. Man have the wife and take her to Patpong. This girl want to make like special for husband. This husband have to fuck Thai girl and Thai girl have to (she sticks out her tongue) this wife. My friend go. I say, "Why?" She say, "Because farang pay me good money, about 5,000 baht only one night. From Germany."

(do some bar girls secretly continue working in Patpong after marrying a foreigner?)

Yeah, I don't know what they think. I don't think she loves the boyfriend. Maybe she think it not enough man for her, she have to fuck and fuck. Me, I think I have a good one. I never do like this. I stop working one year already. It's a long time. I can have a man every night for sure. They try, ask me every night. I say, "I don't want to do that. No good." My girlfriend marry man from Scandinavia and she come back holiday to

Thailand and I know what she do, she fuck around. I tell her, "If you old, you get nothing for sure if you lie like this." Many girl is stupid. That's why I don't like them. They speaking always is bullshit.

≈ ≈ ≈

Darling,

Friday afternoon, 4.30 P.M., sitting in my office. For the first time since I came back to France, I have a little time to write you this short letter. I hope you have seen my friend and you have got the money and letter I gave him for you.

I have been working too much since I came back, both in my office (about 12 hours every day) and at home, because my roommates are not very good in housekeeping, and I have to do most of the work (cleaning, washing, buying and cooking food) this is why I could not find a minute to write to you. Things are getting better now, and I shall write a little more, and maybe give you English reading and writing lessons by letter (I am currently working on this: first letter will be the English alphabet...)

You cannot imagine how much I miss you. My first thought when I wake up in the morning is for you. I say "Hello darling! Good morning!" And the last one, when I go to bed at night, is for you too: "Good night darling, have nice dreams!" When I close my eyes, anytime during the day, I see your face.

I look forward to the moment we will meet again with very much impatience. Time is going too slow when I am away from you, and too fast when I am with you.

Sometimes, when I walk in the street and look at the people, I feel very unhappy: all the people are walking with the ones they love, having fun together, doing every little thing together, and you are so far away! Most of my friends are couples too, and I get jealous sometimes.

Soon, though, I will be with you again, and I would like it to be forever, although I know that it will probably be impossible this time, and that we will have to wait a little longer.

ð𝒶 ð𝒶 ð𝒶

To my Darling,

Just another letter to follow the first letter just in case it went astray. Well darling I have been away from you for 2 weeks now, but it seems like 2 years because I miss you & love you very much, more so because I'm away from you. I hope and want you to feel the same way about me also. Please let me know how you feel about me. I have put the money in your bank a/c which you should have by now. I only hope the next few days & months go quick so I can be with you again soon. Also darling I want to talk to you about coming to Australia when I see you. I hope you are OK & not sick because I can't look after you.

I have been very busy at work & had to work 6 days the first week to catch up on my work, but I have just about caught up now.

I still have restless nights not being able to sleep because I have been thinking of you day & night.

I have got one of you photos in my office to look at, the other photos came out good. The men & women at work said I was lucky to meet someone like you, and so nice a girl as you. Well darling this is all for now, hoping I get a letter soon.

All my love to you forever

x x x x x x
P.S. <u>This</u> letter is not bullshit darling, it <u>is</u> the truth.

❧ ❧ ❧

Darling,

You are wondering who this letter is from.

I'm the English person you met last month. You came back to my hotel 2 times (River City Guest House).

The first time you came back you left in the middle of the night when that other girl came back and was angry with me, she wanted to fight me. Do you remember who I am now?

I went to Phuket after the second day with my two friends.

I was in Bangkok again 10 days after and I looked for you in the Kings Lounge Disco but you were not there.

❧ ❧ ❧

Darling,

I have some important news to tell you, so please make sure you understand this letter. Please take my letter to a translation service if you cannot understand the English. The translation service will write the letter in Thai for you.

<u>Important for you</u>.

I went to see my doctor today to check for any disease I may have caught in Thailand. I explained that I had made love to you many times. Although I could not see anything nasty on my penis ("dick"), my doctor said I may have a very slight infection (non-specific urethritis). He gave me some antibiotic tablets (medicine) to take but told me not to worry. My doctor wanted to be very safe to make sure I do not catch anything nasty. I feel fine, darling, so do not worry and I cannot see any problem. I do not have any pain. I told my doctor I did not use a condom when making love to you. He said I was very foolish and that you were very foolish also. (Make sure when you go with a customer that he wears a condom <u>always</u>.)

Please darling understand that it is <u>very important</u> for you to tell your doctor everything I have written in this letter. <u>Please see your doctor very soon and let him examine you to make sure you have not caught any disease</u> (non-specific urethritis).

I care for you very much and I do not want you to have problems with an infection of your vagina ("pussy"). <u>So please go to see your doctor immediately</u>. I think there is very little for you to worry about—so <u>do not worry</u>. But it is good for you to let your doctor know <u>everything</u>. When I came to Thailand last time, I did not have any disease. My doctor told me I did not have any disease then. I think all is well for me now so when Hubert says <u>be careful</u>, I mean:

1. Make sure customer <u>ALWAYS</u> wears a condom when making love.

2. Do not suck customer and <u>do not</u> let him suck you.

3. Do not take any "ganja" yourself (do not smoke it) and do not carry "ganja" for customer. If you get caught by police, you will be sent to prison for a long time.

Please darling, <u>do not take the risk</u>.

4. Do not have too many Mekong—very bad for your head and liver!

So, <u>please be careful</u>.

Do not take big risks to make extra money.

I hope you understand this.

But darling, I want to be with you again and I hope you feel the same about me.

I hope you get your presents safely. Please write to me to tell me. I have sent you a koala (doll) from Australia to keep you company in your room.

I do not have girlfriends in Australia. I do not like Australian women very much.

But darling I love very much, believe me.

Please take much care darling, especially if you make love with another man (up to you). Make sure:

1. He uses condom (for making love or sucking).

2. Do not let him lick your pussy.

This way, you will be safe. It was safe with me because Hubert does not have any disease. Please understand, darling, about "AIDS." If you catch this disease you will die. So ask your doctor to tell you so you make sure you do not catch "AIDS."

I would be very, very sad if anything bad happened to you. So take care. I hope to see you again, soon. Lots of love.

❧ ❧ ❧

Hello, my Darling!

How are you?

I know, I write too much letters to you, but I hope you change all my letters in Thai language what I have written to you. I think it's very important, I want that you change all my letters, please. I want that you understand me and that you answer all letters, please.

Darling, sure in three months I come in Bangkok to see you and I want that you come with me. I know, it's your life and if you don't like to come with me I must stop staying with you, but I don't want to stop staying with you, I want that you come to me.

Darling, I'm missing you so much and you know, I have started to love you so much and I don't want stop loving you, I want to love you much more. I think, you will understand me when I tell you, I cannot think in love to you when I know that you fuck men, my heart is crying and my soul is suffering so much and I cannot really be happy in my life. I hope you will understand me when I say I must find a way to be happy in my life and maybe you can be happy with me. I told you, you are the first girl who I ask so much time come to Germany and sure in three month I come in Bangkok and if you don't like to come with me, I will never ask you again. But sure when I must stop you, I have broken heart and I must look for a girl, who can to comfort my heart and I think it is not so easy to find. I love you.....

OK. I told you enough about my love to you and I want talk about you.

I think, if you really want to come to me you must change your life. I think, you must start very quickly to learn to write and speak the A.B.C. in English. I know, you much lazy to learn English but I think, you can "do it" to learn every day A.B.C. to write and to speak, please. You can talk to your friend from the room 202 (I'm sorry, I forget the name) maybe you can stay with this girl and you can stop your flat so you have more time to learn and you don't need to work so much, maybe you can stay with your friend and she can help you to learn. I want send some money to you if you really want to learn and I'm a little happy when I know that you don't work.

When you stay with me you have never work for money, I look for you and me all time.

I know, I push you so much, but we have only three month and I want that you start to learn and I want that you stop to make fuck for fuck money. Please, start to learn, "do it" for you and me, I love you so much and I want to stay with you a long time. Don't forget, I think in love to you and don't want stop loving you, but my soul is suffering and any time when I see that I cannot stay with you, I must stop my love to you. I think and I hope you will understand me.

And I'm sure three month no problem for you to learn A.B.C. in English.

Darling, I love you.

⁊ ⁊ ⁊

Darling,

My time in Bangkok was made so wonderful and enchanting by meeting you, and although we met in odd circumstances, I had the best time I've ever had abroad with you. Not only are you beautiful, but a delight to be with as well—I miss you already.

If we had only had more time together, perhaps I could have learned more Thai and you could have learned more English. Indeed, we had trouble with the language barrier, but our communication was one of far deeper meaning: one of emotion. I am patiently, although confused, looking forward to our next meeting, be it in England or Thailand.

I have returned to work, and also study. I'll be in the United States for a few months, when I leave to study in England. I've also enclosed a picture, I hope it suits you, I have your beautiful face hung on my wall.

Please take care of yourself, be careful, and say hello to our friend where you work. Write me soon—I miss your smile.

Love.

⁊ ⁊ ⁊

Darling,

It's nice you remember me. You are a very beautiful lady, darling, and you hurry up and get a husband to love you forever.

Still owe you for that drink I won't forget it. When I left Bangkok, went to Singapore, then to Manila to stay with friends. Had a good time there, then back to Sydney, Australia to my job. You'd like it over in Australia and New Zealand, a haircut for a man cost $10 (= to 120 baht) so you'd make plenty, and meet plenty of men. Hope the lucky one would be me.

I know some Thai people here married to guys. Guess that's what we all want, long time love. You are a very pretty lady darling very sexy ways and bet you are good fucker. I am a big man, my cock is big and is looking for a Thai wife to fuck forever and have a baby.

Have my own house here and work very hard. There's quite a few Asian people here now and many Thai restaurants. Tell me more of your life, darling. I'll be over in Thailand again for a longer time. So will find what I want. Hope I see you, I think I will.

What's the weather like in July, August, there in Thailand, not too much rain? There and Australia are close and a good place it is but come over darling. Please, and let one man enjoy you and take care of you. And kiss your pretty sexy body all over.

OK darling, please write soon and C'mon over.

ک ک ک

My beloved lady,

I was really happy to talk to you on the phone today. It is really wonderful to hear your voice. I miss you so much!

Fortunately, I'll see you within about 45 days now, as I should arrive in Bangkok then if everything goes all right. I already bought my plane ticket, and my friend will go very soon to the Thai Embassy in France to get our visas (for her, her friend and me). We will be together again very soon.

I am glad to know that you are OK. As for myself, I have not been very lucky lately: I currently suffer a golden oriole on my right eye, and a gumboil under one of my teeth. These are mild diseases, but quite painful, especially because both come at the same time! I have a good treatment and it is getting better.

I'd rather be with you in Thailand right now, even if it is rainy season now. The weather in France is not bad, but the sun does not show very much, and I feel so very lonely, because you are so far away from me. It is not very nice to go to bed alone every night. I always think a lot about you, every hour, but especially at night, waiting to fall asleep in my humble room, so far away from the one I love, so lonely.

45 days to wait yet, 44 days tomorrow....such a long time before we get together again!

I went to my bank today and sent you about B 24,000. Money should be on your account by Friday or next Monday. I hope there will be no problem. Please keep me advised.

I shall try to call you next week, if I can get the line!

I love you so very much that words cannot tell.

I hope you will never forget me.

I send you all my love and millions of kisses. See you soon.

Yours, loving.

ᢀ ᢀ ᢀ

(She's wearing jeans and a sleeveless top which displays a tattoo of a marijuana leaf on her upper left arm. A white rabbit's foot good-luck charm dangles from her belt near her crotch. She looks tough with her hair pulled back in a pony tail emphasizing her wizened face. But when her thin lips smile, she appears friendly.)

I work bars more than 25 years. Now I'm 40. I started when 14. I miss the Americans from Vietnam War. I still like. Know why? He Yankee, he just play, make Thai woman happy. When people see me work, everybody say, "Suzy Wong with Yankee," but I don't care. He work with the war. Sweet, nice, can make have a baby. My momma ask me, "How you like him?" I say, "I like him. Very nice." I never talk about the money, never say, "Hey, you got to give me money." I just get 90 baht. My family poor. 90 baht for one day OK. He so sweet. OK, sometime he get drunk, mouth make crazy. He have to work with gun. With war. Have to see hard thing. I don't make him crazy. I say, "Please don't tell me about when you go to the war. I worry." My husband White Horse, he's army. White Horse is the bomb. Bomb! When fighting, he always take the B-52. If you die, you die. He bring me one day to look. B-52. Wheeeeeeeeeeeeeeeeeeeee! Big! I pregnant about three month. When American have to leave, I remember, everybody cry. Some girl have three baby, some girl have two baby. Marry. American Embassy not give the visa yet. You have to wait. You don't know when you get to go. I go in B-52 with my husband. Drive! (She puts her hands on an invisible steering wheel). It on the ground, not in air.

(how did you start working at 14?)

I still like to have money. My friend say, "OK, come with me. You bring flower, sell farang night time." Is good. When I sell the flower, I 13. For one year. When I 14, can go in the bar. I see one guy, my husband, he look at me. He ask me, "Hey, girl, you work in bar?" I say, "No no no no no. I sell flower. Want to buy?" I say, "10 baht." He speak with one guy at the bar, this 1965, then he take me to the hotel. I still scared you know. I sleep with him the night. He know I virgin. He know already I virgin. One guy work in the bar, know, say to him, "Hey, careful man. She a virgin. Thai custom when you fuck with the girl who virgin, you go to the jail." He scared. I say, "The last night you sleep with me, you hold me. Why you don't make fuck?" He say, "I take you see your momma." Me I don't care. "Come on. I take you see my momma, but I tell you one thing, I very poor." You know what he say to momma? "I want to get married with she." My mom don't understand. I have to say her. I stay with him, marry with him. One baby. I have card, I can buy anything from the shop. PX. Three year together. Everything is good. Later he say, "I tell you one thing I know you don't want to hear." I say, "What? You my husband, I your wife." He say, "You and me have to finish." I say, "Why you say like this? I never go out, I stay home with my baby. Make food." He say, "Yankee have to go back." He say, "Yankee, Thailand, everything is shit." I say, "No, you don't have to go."

(how did other bar girls react when their boyfriends or husbands finished their military tours of duty in Southeast Asia?)

My girlfriend hang neck. She marry with my husband friend. Still pregnant. She 22. Too young. Two baby. You know how many small Yankee baby in Thailand? 400, 500 Yankee. Very poor. I see some nigger baby just in the market, begging, "Can I have one baht?" I say, "Oh, oh." In America, I stay, everything good. Why America is big money, no come to Thailand pick up babies? Yeah, some Thai lady fuck with farang, fuck with America. Have to take baby back to America. After he go back, I come in San Francisco. Six months. Very nice. One baby hold and one baby pregnant. I come back Thailand, baby born. Husband in San Francisco buy big motorcycle. Harley. Big one. Big! I say, "Now you got house, car, I still with you."

When I come back to Bangkok, I get phone call, "You have to fly back, your husband accident with the motorbike." When he die, I become crazy. I stay hospital crazy three month in Bangkok. I crazy. When he die there, I don't care. I drink, drink. My mother-in-law have to send me back. I don't know anything. I don't know my mother, I don't know my baby. I stay in crazy hospital three months. When I get out, I get in the jail a year and six months because my mother said, "I see one Thai people slap a farang." I pick the bottle and broke him on the head, then I put up knife (she gestures as if stabbing someone in the stomach.) The police found me.

When I come out I start work in bar because my father die and no one take care my mother. I have to do it. I don't want to do it. I about 20 years old. 1971. Petchburi Road. I no more fall in love. I only fall in love with the money. My heart is hurt already. Yeah, I can say, "I love you! I love you!" to a thousand farang. Morning time come, "500 baht! Finish!" I need money. Everybody need money.

(what do you think of today's younger generation of bar girls?)

Maybe likes money. Too young. Only buy clothes. Buy shoes. I see the young girls. They call me sister. I see they spend money. Two hours, 4,000 to 5,000 baht. For me, I spend same money for month, or more. I tell every girl I meet, "When I was Suzy Wong, I go with the man, I get 90 baht, 200 baht. Altogether one night I get 290 baht. I work very hard, more than you. You work good." She say, "Crazy." I say, "Yeah, today everything expensive." Before, two egg just one baht. Now two egg five baht. Now cook with rice, everything, 10 baht, 15 baht. Before, five baht cook rice everything. I tell the girl, "That's your life. No good. You're young. Maybe you can find shop. Maybe you want more money?" I talk with the young girl, "When you work, keep your money. When you don't keep your money, you like me." She say, "Want to work, want nice clothes." She don't want to listen. OK, that's her pussy, not mine. "Be careful AIDS."

When I go Patpong now, I never know the girls. Today, they just make happy, fun. Today tourist. My time, G.I. stay together you. Never pay you. Like boyfriend-girlfriend. They pay the room, food. Good life. More than now. Now only drink and fuck. Tourist just come holiday, spend their money. It's nothing. G.I. come Vietnam, have girlfriend, go holiday with girlfriend. Vietnam day was better. I not like one night, two night or one month, two month. Or some night nothing. Sometimes boring, sometimes good. With G.I., stay together longer, longer. More, more. When someone talk, "Yankee bad," you know what I feel? Then I stop. I don't want to go back crazy again.

I have America passport. I not divorced. My husband die. I'm first woman from the slum, Pratunam, to go to America with the farang G.I. I'm the first one. I'm a Suzy Wong.

Today I do nothing. I open the shop. I sell some rice, some eggs, some oil in Pratunam, in the slum. I like to make money with the shop. It's good. Everybody look me higher. When I work the bar girl, yeah, you have good money but no one look at you higher.

(what are the different nationalities of men like?)

English, from England, is his style. When he want to take woman, they don't ask, "You Suzy Wong? How much?" They just say, "OK, I take you. Bring you the dinner tonight." He never say, "You have to go sleep with me." He like me to be higher too. German, when he drunk, say always, "Fuck! Shizer! You just make pussy! 500 baht! Finish!" Fighting talk. At the table, shouting, "Get away! Ahhhhhhhhgh! Fuck you! I pay you money, get away!" German say when wake up, "Hey! Fuck you steal my money!" More junkie, more drug. Before all American drug. Now American clean. All clean. You see in Thailand, German all junkie. And he look the bar girl like animal (she makes a claw with her right hand). The bar girl be animal girl with animal farang.

Yankee, very clever. Very smart. Please Thai woman. Say, "Thai woman very sweet." Very much Thai custom. He make like Thai style. (She places her hands together in the prayer position to demonstrate a traditional, respectful Thai "wai" greeting.) He never say, "You fuck off." Japanese, very hard. When they like someone, just keep, to be with them, only him and her. But I don't know, I never sleep with Japanese. Australia only sweet guy, "Hey mate!" Canada, some very angry too much when he don't like. Say very bad thing. But Canada is OK. I more hate German. America number one.

(are Thai men attracted to foreign women the way foreign men are attracted to Thai ladies?)

I hear Thai men talk, they like to be with the farang lady but her skin like the frog. Farang lady skin, no good skin. Very soft. And farang lady hole is very big. Thai woman, have two, three baby, hole is no very big. But farang lady, hole not have the baby is very big.

Farang lady give blow job too. Thai man cannot find Thai lady give the blow job. Thai man say, "Farang lady give the blow job. I want to find the farang lady give the blow job. But skin like the frog!" Before, I don't know about blow job. Then the war. Now many girl know a lot. Do! Do!

(any unusual experiences with foreign men?)

I get one crazy guy. He sleep with me. When he like to come, he tell me, "I have to come now!" I have to bite him everywhere his body. Hard. He say, "More!" When I turn on the light, I see he cut all his arm, all his back from bite. But he have good cream. He can never wear the short shirt, short pants. He old man. Dirty.

❧ ❧ ❧

Darling,

How are your girl friends (Kuay may men!), Noy (bright girl "Fuck you"), Young Sister and husband, and your cousins? Give them my love. I love them all! Oh, I almost forgot that very ugly, not bright girl—what's her name—Ummmmm.....Oh yes you—Yat Sister, very juk jik!!

Darling, only joking. I love you very much, and although you are half a world away from me, you are in my heart and thoughts, constantly; I cannot wait to see you again; my bed is very cold and lonely.

Cuddlee Wuddlee Baby.

Write soon.

Love & kisses & Cuddlee Wuddlee

❧ ❧ ❧

My dearest lady,

I am very very tired these days, because I did not sleep much lately: I worry too much about you. I am very sad that you hung up the telephone on me two nights ago (it was 4.30 AM in France).

I feel you were very angry with me and it makes me feel very bad, because I love you so very much and think of you every second of my life, and that I always do my to make things easy and nice for the both of us. I tried to call you back later that day, but you were not there.

Oh my only one, you know I only wish the best for you and I will always work the hardest to make it so, until my latest breath.

Please do not be angry with me because it hurts me so bad I cannot tell. <u>You are my only hope,</u> the only person I can live and fight for.

It is true, my love: if it was not for you, I would feel a very old and tired man, a useless person, and would eventually give up everything and let myself die. <u>I have nobody else than you.</u>

Please, my love, do not forget me. Please forgive my sins, my clumsiness and my weakness.

Write me a few words, or give me a telephone call, because your love is as important and vital to me as the air I breathe or the water I drink and I could not live without you.

I love you and will always do. I shall never forget you, nor let you down.

Please love me a little.

Truly yours.

                  ❧ ❧ ❧

My Darling,

I just had to write again to you because I still miss you very much & love you I am waiting for your letter then I will send you some more money. I hope you are OK & missing me as much as I do I just want to be with you all the time now. Because I really feel so much for you. I have been working 6 days a week because we are busy but I told the manager that I was taking a week off from work soon I only hope it goes fast so as I can be there once again with you. This is all for now darling I feel a lot better when I write to you especially when I can express my feelings on paper.

I love you & always will.

Missing you also.

Teelak. x x x

x x x x

❧ ❧ ❧

Hello Darling!

How are you? I'm O.K. now. I start to work again and the pain in my finger goes away. Now I'm sitting in the kitchen room and I look the football game England against Netherlands and later we go in a discotheque.

I hope you come to Germany soon because I miss you so much. Try to find your husband to make the divorce and try to get a new passport quickly because summertime is a very good time in Germany, hot the same like Thailand and we can go to Italy and I show you Milano, Rome and some other nice places there.

If you cannot find him, come also soon because I want to see the woman which I love for sure, nothing can change my feeling to you. I was a little bit angry about you because you ask me at the telephone, if I love you for sure, you want to know sure. Don't do that again because I think I show you enough that I love you for sure and that my feelings never can change because I found you, you understand and I need no other woman because I found the woman which I love.

Try to make the divorce and I marry you and you can be sure that I'm better for you than your husband.

I love you very much and I never can give you shit or give you pain. If I don't love you I never do what I do for you now.

My Mama wants that you come soon also and we can go to Church because my friend wants to marry soon; maybe we too!!!

Say a big Hello to Mama and to your family.

P.S: Send me a letter and come to me.

Much Love.

ɜ❧ ɜ❧ ɜ❧

Darling,

You may be surprised to get a letter from the Netherlands. I met you on one month ago about 11 o'clock in the Pussy Galore club. I found you very nice (character and appearance attractive). You gave me your address and I would like to answer you. I enclose a photo of me. Probably and hopefully you can remember me. It is already a long time.

That evening I didn't give you money. I feel very sorry about that. If you like I will send some money or probably something else. Just tell me.

I have not introduced myself. I am 42 years, but I feel myself younger. I do a lot of sports (jogging, tennis) and I work as a bookkeeper in an office. I live in the Netherlands. It is a flat country.

This I would like to tell you: I would very much appreciate if you wrote to me. If you can't answer my letter for one or more reasons, I can understand.

Hopefully I hear something of you.

Kind regards.

Darling,

I know now by the way I feel that I would never treat you that way again. You are more important to me than anything else in my life darling. I don't want to lose you, for any reasons.

I am very afraid now, that maybe I already have.

I wish that I could have been with you there longer to try to show you how I really feel about you.

It hurts me that I am unable to do that.

What will you remember about me now darling? Did I push any chance for us being happy together farther away? I want to live deep in your heart darling, not on the other side of the world. I don't want to lose touch with you. Why is it so easy for you to put me aside that way? I am very unhappy without you close to me. Don't you feel the same way as me?

How many more times will you ask me to wait? I know seven months is not a long time, and maybe it is better for both of us to take our time with each other, but why didn't you tell me? Why didn't you let me know more about what you wanted to do?

It seems to me now that you are putting me off because your thoughts of me have changed.

What do you want me to think now darling?

I know you didn't know what to expect of me before. I should have made more of an effort to let you know. I'm sorry I couldn't get back as soon as I said I would. I

102

didn't realize that would happen. Now that you know I will come back for you from any distance, what are you going to do this time?

How do you think it makes me feel knowing that I'm not the only one you are considering. The only thing I can do is pray that it will be me. That is one reason why I wanted to see the Emerald Buddha with you. When you didn't want to, I felt that you didn't care.

I know that you are young and you are trying to choose what is best for you in your life. I can only ask if I can be a part of it with you. I want to do everything I can to make a difference in your life. To try to take care of the things that are most important to you. I understand what they are. Teach me more darling. I want your love and I want to make you happy. I want you to be happy with me.

Why did you have to say to me that you are not the same as me because you cannot stay away from your family the way I have?

It hurts me that I don't see them as often as I would like to. It is not easy for me darling. I love them but I also love you. That is why I wanted to see you first. Because they cannot give to me the same type of love that I have being with you. That is something I always want to have with me. I want to keep the kind of love I have for you. When it is time, I want to have my own family. I want to have that with you.

It was very special to me going to northern Thailand to meet your family. I felt that I was a part of you like never before and I want to share more times with you like that. It was a beautiful experience and it made me very happy to be with you and your family that way.

Please don't take away from us being there together. I want to be the only one to have done that with you.

Maybe this is a good time for you to decide darling, what is it that you want most in your life? Stop what you do and think about that. I want more than anything else to spend it with you. I don't want any more time to be free, because I know I never will be if I don't keep inside of me what I believe I need for happiness in this life. Both of us want to get away from the things we have to do. I want everything to be better for us. Let's do it together darling. It would be a way of protecting each other.

I know I didn't make it sound good to you because of my job and the amount of money I have. But I would have no problem taking care of you. I wanted to know if you loved me before anything else. You have to believe and trust me darling that I can make you happy. Please do not worry about that. I don't want it to stop us from ever knowing what it would be like together.

If you think we have a future to share, I want to make plans with you. Tell me what it is you would like to do. It is a good time to plan things now. I am willing to do many different things with you. But I want you to help me decide for the both of us. I don't care if it's in America or Thailand. I would be happy as long as it was with you.

"I love you very much darling." They are not just words to me when I say it to you. Please don't forget me anymore. How will you be able to understand if you love me if you never wait alone for me?

Give it a chance darling. If you cannot be faithful now, will you ever be?

It is a dream to be married to you. And I pray that when I come back, it will happen. We have to give of each other more so it can.

I will know if it is what you really want before I go. Because I will be able to feel it. I think about you every day and I often wake up at nights doing the same. I guess it must be up to you because I already know that I want it with you.

Please tell me about the things you know I want to hear more about. I wouldn't care if you were communist. If you loved me, that is all that matters to me.

Don't hide from me darling. What good is that going to do us? We have to begin somewhere. Let's start now.

That is all I can say for now. Take care of yourself and tell me what the doctor did for your eyes. Did you go yet?

Write back to me as soon as you can. I am looking forward to it.

Love You Always...

Love.

ta ta ta

My Darling,

How can I put into words how much I love you. I now know my love for you will last forever. You are now my wife and when I put the wedding ring on your finger it made me so happy that you have accepted my love.

We both have to accept the fact that things will not be easy for us. If you love me as I love you, it will make things a lot easier for both of us to be together and stay together till death do us part.

I so much enjoyed the time we last spent together and I know now our love for each other is for real. I hope and pray that I can see you very soon and replenish our love for each other. Look after our daughter because she will also be part of our lives when we are together again.

I know sometimes I drink too much but it is only because I am so lonely and miss you so much. My heart and my body is only for you forever. I "love" you so much, perhaps with all my heart I "love" you too much.

Please have faith in my love for you. I need you so much to make my life start all over again.

I still cannot believe that I fell in love with so beautiful Thai girl who makes my heart so happy whenever I think of you.

I wear your pendants so close to my heart all the time, I kiss them, I cherish them with all the feelings my heart can give. I now feel so sad and tears are in my eyes because of my "love" for you. I "love" you so much.

Okay my love now at this moment I am about to cook myself a meal. It is one of my favourite meals. Steak, chips and mushrooms. When we are finally together I will teach you how to cook Australian food. Perhaps you will enjoy too.

But remember you must cook for me Thai food that we will both enjoy.

I must go now because to write much more will only make me more sadder because I think of you so much. "I LOVE YOU"

"Please Don't Forget To Remember Me." Your Loving Husband x x x x x x x

x x x x x x I wish my body was close to you. I really love you forever.

෴ ෴ ෴

(Dressed in a low-cut blouse to show off her attractive cleavage, a 28-year-old transsexual sits on a barstool at a tiny, outdoor bar along Patpong Road. She was a man until an operation changed his sex. In Thailand, a transsexual is called a "katoy" or "lady-man.")

I had operation two years ago because I like to be woman. I don't know why. I born like this. Operation cost 45,000 baht for cut here (she gives a sharp karate chop to her genitals), 20,000 baht for breasts and 8,000 baht for nose. The doctor ask my age, have VD or not and if clean. If clean, they can change a person. I have operation in Thonburi Hospital. The hospital is OK, there is good doctor there. They ask why you want be woman. I say, "I like." I have to sign my name so if I die they have no problem. There are a lot of katoy in Thailand because katoy good idea, and good take care service for customer, and nice looking woman, nice body. Thai men have no hair, not same European have hair (she points to the body hair on a nearby foreigner's forearm.) Thai easy to look nice katoy, modern woman.

(have you ever fallen in love with a foreign customer?)

Someone before. I have one boyfriend, love very much. He is Canadian. He have wife, so he cannot live with me, cannot come to me many time. He don't know me I'm a boy before. I no tell.

(do you usually keep this secret from your clients?)

If they ask, OK. If they don't ask, they don't know. Of 100, about 10 people know.

❧ ❧ ❧

To my Darling,

Just a follow on letter to my other 2 letters which I hope you got OK. I just want to keep writing to you. Because you are still so much in my heart & body that I must write to you. Again. But I don't want replies to all my letters I only want you to write when you can. & say that you miss me & love me as much as I do.

Darling in my 2nd letter I said about you coming to Australia which I said I would talk to you soon about it.

107

But what I meant darling that I would like to bring you over to Australia soon for a few weeks to let you see what it is like over here because as you know a lot of Thai girls get married & go to other countries & it doesn't work out and they return to Thailand. But I want you to see Australia first & then decide if you like it here. Then I can start seeing about us getting married that's if you still want me then. I will finish up now. Hoping & waiting for your letter to arrive. Because it seems like months since I have been away from you.

Love you forever.

🐲 🐲 🐲

Hello Darling,

It is me again missing you & loving you just as much as ever. It was lovely to hear your voice over the phone on Friday night it made me feel a lot better, but I will ring again Friday week at the same time. Please write to me only if it is a few words. Get your teacher to help you & I will bring her a present over when I come. I just want a reply to some of my letters to see how you feel about me. And when I receive your letter I will send you some more money. So please write darling. I hope you like getting all these letters but I love writing to say what is in my mind & body because it builds up inside of me every day because being away from you really hurts. I am hoping the next few months goes quick so as I can be with you once again. This is all for now. I will be <u>waiting for your letter</u>

All my love & kisses.

x x x x

🐲 🐲 🐲

Hello my mosquito!

I hope you are fine? I'm very sorry that I have not written before but I have been very busy. I have worked every day to get money to make it possible come back to Thailand as soon as possible. Maybe next week? Nobody knows.

I want to thank you very much for your letter and postcard and especially a crocodile doll. I like it very much. It sleeps every night with me. Only me and my crocodile doll. I don't know with whom you sleep. Maybe you sleep with your Japanese boyfriend??? Or with your lover—chocolate man! I cannot be sure because you butterfly too much.

Nevermind—I still love you.

In your postcard you said that you are sick. I hope it is not serious and you are now healthy. If not you must go to doctor and take care of yourself.

I have tried to find pictures of my family but I have not been successful. But if I find something I promise to send it to you (my mosquito).

Now I must ask your help. Can you ask somebody what I have to do if I come to Bangkok to drive tuk-tuk. I am serious because that is my biggest dream in the world. Because I know Bangkok very well (I am not joking) I think that I have very good chances to manage in the traffic of Bangkok. I am waiting for your opinion about my plannings (don't laugh at me).

It has happened nothing wonderful in Finland. The winter has almost gone and the summer is coming soon. I think that the summer is also coming to your city (small city) and then it is very hot (it is always hot in Bangkok?)

Now I must finish because I am very tired. One reason is also that the crocodile doll is waiting for me to come sleep and I don't want to make it angry. I hope that you will get this short letter and some day you have time to write me and tell what is going on in Thailand. I will write you later. Good luck for you!

Love.

P.S. You are every day on my mind!

ها ها ها

Hello, my Darling!

How are you?

I hope everything is O.K. to you my Thai girl.

I cannot write so much, because it is so late in the evening and I must work tomorrow.

The last letter to me made me very happy and I want to say thank you and I'm very glad to see you in Bangkok.

I must tell about something and I hope you are not angry to me, but I want that you stop to stay with a man some days before I come to Bangkok and that you check you body about A.I.D.S. and I want to see this in English language.

Sorry so much my darling, but I hope you will try to understand me.

Don't forget I like you very much and I want to stay with you some weeks if you like too.

Soon I'm coming and I hope you stay at your apartment too waiting for me, I want to phone to you sure. Don't forget me!

in love.

P.S. Don't be angry my darling, I like you.....

ها ها ها

Darling,

Thank you for writing to me. I didn't think that you were going to do that because you were mad at me. Please don't stop now because of the way things are.

These are pictures of where I was looking forward to taking you in America. My father sent them to me so that I can show you. It's where he lives now.

I thought you might like it here because of the weather. It's warm all year round as it is in Thailand. There are many things that I would like to do with you here. I wanted you to see it so that you can decide if you want to stay and live with me here. Maybe you would like it. I have a good-paying job refueling aircraft at the airports waiting for me next year, when I am no longer in the military. But I don't know if I am going to take it yet.

It's good to hear that your eyes are going to be fine. They are very pretty and I like to look into them. I wish that I could see you now.

My brother and his wife recently had a new baby. I am very happy for them, but it also makes me feel sad because I wish that it could have been me.

Is that another reason why you are unsure that you want to marry me darling? You do not know if you want to have a baby with me? I know that I am not everything you like in a man, but I don't feel that way about you. How much you love me is the only thing I care about.

I know you are angry at me because I did not keep my promise to send you money. It is not because I don't care about you anymore. It was required of me to pay off all of my bills, and that is what I had to do.

There are more problems we are having with the Arabs again, and by the time you receive this letter, I will be in a country called, "Saudi Arabia." I have to fly their soon. Watch the news on T.V. and you will understand more. My mother worried when I told her I have to go. She has not seen me in a long time, and now she thinks she never will. I told her not to worry because I want to go. It will pass time for me before I

111

return to Bangkok to see you. I don't think I will still be there in 6 months unless there is a war.

I am sorry about this darling. It's why I don't want this job anymore. I move around too much. That is why I wanted to get a bank account with you. I could have sent money to you by allotment and there would be no problem. I wish that you would trust my intentions more. I was not trying to be selfish with you. I have my reasons for wanting to do things a certain way. I wish that you would understand that more. Now you are going to think I don't care about your situation. That is not true darling. Please don't get that idea. I want to help you with that. That is why I was being demanding with you before. To try and make you understand that I want to help you. I felt afraid and impatient that I would not have enough time with you. Two weeks is not much for that.

I know I went about it the wrong way darling, but now I have no way at all to convince you of my intentions. I always worry that it will go unnoticed, and unexpressed, because of the distance between us, and the way things are now. How are you going to know and understand that now darling? I am not going to be able to send you money from a foreign country. I hope that you can understand my situation also.

I don't want this to be the end of what we have started darling. Is that what it means to you? I know it is important, but I would like to think there is more to our relationship than what we can do for each other. I understand more now that you cannot rely on me for money and that you will have to go to work. It hurts me that you resort to that. It is not the way of life that I want you to have. You deserve better. You are too good for it and worth more than that. I wish that you would feel that way about yourself, and not simply do it for spite. I am sorry that I was furious with you before darling. But how would you feel if I didn't care at all? Doesn't that matter to you?

Your love is very valuable to me darling. We can't stop everything every time there is a problem. If you are really thinking of marriage with me it is important for us to continue, or we may never know how we feel about each other. If this is what you want to do also, we have to try and help with that more. My love for you will never go away or fade if you don't want it to, but neither will the things that we do not want to discuss and keep a secret. If we are both serious about each other, and the plans we have, that will not be a healthy way for us to continue. I want to trust each other together and at the same time darling. Not wait for one of us to start, or do it first. How are we going to know how much we love each other if we do that? You say you are waiting for the day that we can understand each other. I wish you would consider me enough for that also. Avoiding it will only get in the way of our emotions and feelings for each other darling. That is a waste of time, and I hope that we can do better than that, "now," and when I return to see you on your birthday.

Why do you still want me to wait until you are of legal age (20) before I go back to Thailand? Why don't you want to tell me about that? I know you don't owe me any explanations darling, but that is not why I want you to tell me more. I want you to know that I will still have love for you and that I will understand.

Please give me a chance to show you that.

Do you have obligations until then?

I also want you to know that it is the way you really are that I love darling. Not the way you think you have to be to get what you want. I understand your situation and what you are concerned about, but it's still up to you how you want to be. You are the only one that you

113

should ask about that. You are very beautiful and warm, both inside and out, and I don't want to see you forget that.

I really do wish for us to continue writing each other darling. You can still send it to this address. The military will know where to send it from there.

My love for you will last as long as yours does for me. I hope and pray that it will be forever.

The money I am saving will be for us if it is meant for us to be together. I am willing to do whatever you want to be happy. Maybe you will know more when I return. If anything changes during this time, please let me know. I don't want you to hurt me as you did before. It takes a long time for it to go away.

Please take good care of yourself. I Love You Darling,

Whatever you do, don't forget that. I'll call you as soon as I can. & send money too. O.K. Love x x x x x x x

☙ ☙ ☙

Dear Darling,

I am happy to write this letter because I want to say that I love you. When I was in Bangkok for such a short time I did not tell you enough how much I love you.

These short holidays with my friends are not good for you and me because there is too much drinking and not enough loving. Please forgive me my love.

I'm sorry also that I took a girl to the Suriwong but it hurt me very much to see you acting like a bar girl in the Tavern Bar last Sunday morning and after that I did not care about anything. I asked you many times to stop this cheap behaviour.

I enclose some money and will send the telephone bill tomorrow.

I have decided that next time I come to Bangkok we will go to Koh Samet and also either Phuket or Hua Hin.

114

I am now very busy at work and although I think about you all the time you are such a long way from my arms.

My friend leaves Saudi tomorrow for his new job. We have worked together for 10 years.

I don't know why you go to Patpong when I'm not there and you refuse to tell me. I promise you now that if ever you want to tell me something I will be understanding. It is not knowing that makes me sad. You must trust me, my love.

I must finish now. Be happy my darling and take very good care of yourself.

Love you a lot.

❧ ❧ ❧

(She looks tough, angry, as if about to argue. She's stocky, with her full mouth usually in a frown.)

I am 30. First time fall love with man from United States. Two-and-a-half years. Finish. Same time I had Thai husband. American he know but he love me. But after my friend talking to him, make shit, and he make letter say, "Now I know why you sleep me only three nights one week." He want to marry me but say, "I think you love Thai man more." I see him Nana Hotel and say to him, "I have husband, how can I marry? My husband don't give me money. I working." So America say, "OK, finish, my friend." Kiss me one time, give me money and say, "Bye-bye." He best man, United States. When I with him I happy. One year later, my husband die, drink whiskey. I write letter to America but he never send back. I think he get the letter.

Another, Australian, he with me now. He come back soon. Five months I went with him. Him ask me about passport but he never say, "I love you." Him say, "I like you." He never say, "Marry." I say, "I have passport." But he say nothing. I don't know future.

(why did you begin working as a bar girl?)

I have girl friend and play cards. And I see my friend make beautiful and I ask, "What you work?" She say, "Bar." I go King's Castle. No dancing. My work only open the door, open the door. I like when lady make beautiful, have gold. I think she have husband too, she don't care. So I work.

(do you have any children?)

I have one eight-year boy. Some lady gave me. Father from Kuwait. Mother working Grace Hotel, go with Arab. She say, "I don't want this baby," say, "I give you." I think she joke. I take care. Maybe I never have baby before, I feel something. Cute. You know Arab has big eyes. From me, I have one with Thai husband. Now three-year boy.

(do you believe the letters you receive from foreign men?)

I don't believe. Some man stay only one week, two week, how can him say he love me? If he say, "I like you," I believe. I make letter back to him, I say, "My dear, now you go back one month, look like one year. I think if six month, look like six year! I want you come before, quickly. Because I stay with you I happy. I enjoy. Won't you believe me? I never have feelings same before." I want him enjoy when he look letter. Because he work too hard. I say, "I want to send my picture you." I say, "OK honey, I want to sleep and stop my letter but I want you thinking me all the time, same like me, when I eat, when I work. I think you." I be joking, say, "Sometime I sleeping with somebody, I

116

thinking about you too." I say, "Love you too much, love love love love." This I write Australia man.

(do you write things that are not true to other foreign men?)

Sometimes in the letter I not true. In one week man say, "I love you, OK, marry with me." I say, "I look you letter, you want marry to me? Me too! I love you!" Same. Him lie to me first.

(but why lie back to him?)

Because I want him come back to Bangkok so my business good.

(if your customer later goes with other girls, are you angry?)

I angry. But I cannot make fight because man can say, "I come here holiday. Can have any lady."

(when you do fight with a customer, what do you argue about?)

About money. I say, "700 baht." Him say, "400." Before, he say, "700." After, he forget. I shy. Sometimes I have problem about money.

(what nationalities do you like the most?)

I like United States number one. Australia number two, then Canada, then England. Only four countries I like. (she shows a photograph of a 47-year-old Canadian man) This good man, him care about everything. About money.

Take care about food. I stay one week with him. One year ago. Him write, "You now too old, you don't think future. You want to say yes or no and I help you." He don't write about love love love. Only about help me and my baby. I like. Not love. I write one time, just to talk. He send one time 300 dollar. I write letter, "I have problem with my family." Say, "My mother leg no good and want to take out problem in her eye." And he send money. My mother don't know. I lost the money play cards. Poker. Now I stop. Now I want get money for me because I don't have. I send every month 2,000 or 1,500 baht to my mom. No more play cards. I lose everything. Lose time for work. Lose idea too because when I play, I play all day to morning, then all day to morning again. It make me crazy. I think, no more. I don't say finish. But I stop. Before sometimes I lose 1,000, 5,000 baht. I stop 4 months. Because business not good. I worry about business. I want to have business every day. One night I don't get the man, I have big problem. Not for sex. But to pay because one day I borrow 20,000 baht. Have to pay 24,000 baht. 20 percent more.

(will you marry the Australian?)

If him ask me, I have to say yes. He feel something with me, sure. Sure.

(what advice would you give a young girl who is considering whether or not to become a bar girl?)

If she lady, I tell her, "Never work this." If she already fuck around, I say, "Yes, go to work. Better. You enjoy, get money too." Why she make fuck for free? If she come Bangkok to go school, I must help her. I must see the man and say, "How much you pay her?" If she virgin, I must say to her, "No. Work shop, sell shirt, is better." Because if work same me, she get hard heart. She never have money before, now she have money too much. She never have good clothes before, now she have clothes too much. If new girl want to do, sometimes she come and sit behind me. I must see and look first. Maybe she say she never did before. I take three young girl work with me. 17 years old, two lady. And 20 years, one lady. She say never work before. I give the man to her, this man go with me before. I say to man, "I have lady with me. She have problem with money." I give her all the time the man. Is good. Short time. One China man give 500 baht. One farang, from Sweden, give 700 baht. She give me 100 baht. I say, "I don't want money, buy me food." I never take money. She say she need money, why I want to take it?

(is it possible for a Patpong bar girl to meet and marry a foreigner?)

I think easy. I ask my friend. She say, "Happy. After two months I go with man. Go German." I see many lady go. But when they go, they working there. Dancing or work in the bar, like that. Lady stay with man one week, two week, go foreign country. I think for work, not for love. Many young farang man come Bangkok looking for lady, like gigolo. Gigolo German, Sweden. Handsome. Take lady for working. I go with gigolo man from German, but only one night. He give me 500 baht. He say, "I gigolo man from German." I look, I know. Good sex! I have friend marry farang. Happy. Why not? She go Sweden. He send money to family. 80 percent girls happy after marry. They marry for love. For love. They work outside Thailand, too much money. A lot of girls want to go out Thailand and work. The girl dream. Sometimes I dream. Close my eyes. But when open, nothing. I dream, want have the man with me, have money, make family happy, go any place. It only dream. My friend she stay Germany, say, "I have husband in Germany, I happy." But then she know me, she cannot lie. She say, "I love the man gigolo." She work fucking show in Germany. But she love that man too much.

(do some girls marry foreign customers after only a few nights with them?)

Maybe after two or three days sleep with man and man feel something quickly. She will marry. She say quickly, "Yes" because she working for family. So after she there, then she see good or bad.

(what attracts foreign men to Thai women?)

I ask man, "You have your wife, why you come Thailand?" Some man say, "Want different sex. Thai lady do another sex from farang lady." He say, "Yeah, I want Thai girl." When he come here, he free. I go before with farang husband and wife. After husband have feeling sex, he make love with wife, not with me. She make love and I looking! Crazy! Only I do with the man. Only she touch my face. Three days I go with them, do two times sex.

(what is Thai society's reaction to your work?)

Maybe think ugly. Or look, and think no good. Sometimes when Thai man see me with farang in street, he say, "Why not me? Why? Because I not farang?" and make sound (she makes a loud kissing noise). Or he say, "Want to fuck?" I say, "Fuck your mother." He say, "Why? Because Thai man no money?"

❧ ❧ ❧

Darling,

I hope my letter finds you at home. I am worried about you because I do not know where you are. I hope you are safe and well. Please be very careful and do not take any big risks.

I telephoned Rififi Bar again last week but the lady told me you were on holiday. I will telephone Rififi Bar again and try and speak to you.

I am coming back to Bangkok <u>soon</u> so I hope very much to see you again. I hope you will stay with me next time every day and every night.

There is so much I want to talk to you about. But you do not write to me so I do not know what to think.

If you are in trouble, please tell me and I will try to help you. (I hope you do not have any problems—but I want to help you.)

If you change your job or move from your house, please let me know where to contact you. If I arrive in Bangkok and I cannot find you, I will be very, very unhappy.

Later...

I telephoned you tonight at Rififi Bar—I was very pleased to speak to you and to know you are safe and well. I feel much better now. I feel so good to speak to you.

Please believe me, darling, I do not love that other girl. I met her before in Bangkok and she was a friend to me—no more. I do not want to be her lover. So do not worry about her. I want to be with <u>you</u>. I am so unhappy I cannot be with you tonight.

<u>Please write me a little letter</u>, because I worry very much about you. I try to telephone you at Rififi Bar but I do not know where you are. So I worry very much.

Because I care for you, I want to know you are safe and happy.

So please ask man to write letter for you.

I want so much to come back to Thailand and be with you again. I miss you very much. I am coming to Bangkok soon <u>to see you</u>. I do not want any other Thai lady—only you. I do not tell you a lie.

I am very sorry you got so angry when you saw me take the other girl for dinner (last time I came to Bangkok). But, darling, do not be angry, I love only you.

I hope you will send me a little letter and tell me what you really feel about me. I think you like me a little bit but I am not sure. I hope we can stay good friends for ever. But please, darling, understand that I do not have lots of money to give to you. I can only help you a little bit because I have to pay so much money to come to Bangkok on aeroplane. I am not a rich man I am sorry.

When you write to me, tell me you have received the cassette-player I sent you (and 500 baht).

I am keeping fine so do not worry about me. Please be careful yourself and keep away from trouble.

I will bring you some little presents from Australia when I come.

I do want to try to find work in Bangkok so I can live in Thailand.

I am well educated (did you know?)—I hope you will help me to find a job.

I love you very much and I want to be with you.

I do not have any other Thai ladies I am interested in—only you.

So do not worry. Next time I try to find work in Bangkok. I do not take out other ladies to dinner—that is a promise. Also, I do not want to make love to other Thai ladies—only you. I <u>do</u> want to make love to you.

I do not tell a lie about money. I have only medium salary and I have to be careful with money. But I will help you as much as possible. I do not want you to think I am a "Cheap Charlie." It is very expensive to come by aeroplane to Thailand.

However, I want to see you again darling and I hope very much you do not have any problems.

I will try to help you.

I love you very much,

Your friend.

❧ ❧ ❧

(She's wearing bright white lingerie inside a Patpong bar where she has just finished dancing onstage and is now relaxing before it's her turn again. She's looking good—charged, intelligent and in control—but somewhat ravaged.)

I am 29, have been working in Patpong for three years.

(how many letters have you received?)

Too much.

(do you believe them?)

50-50. Sometimes good man. Somebody crazy.

(do you say you love them?)

I say, "Love! Love! Love!" But not. I feel nothing. I say "love" for money. I say "love," but in my heart, nothing. Money! (laughs). One man I love, from Sweden. He very young. Now finish. He go back Sweden. He not write, not very good. I thinking about him. He good man. I want marry the man. I working because I looking marry the man. Good man. Because I don't like Thai man. Thai man think lady work Patpong too much money, go with the farang. Thai man like money from the lady. Farang man give money to lady but Thai man want some money from me. I look good man. He wear nice shirt, not smell bad, not tell lies and not a drunk. Old men, 35 to 40 are good. Young men want fuck for free. Old men understand very good. Young man make love for free, he think about not pay money.

(what do you think about when you make love with them?)

I think about shopping. Shopping for gold. Or I think nothing. I don't like. It's not fun.

(what do foreign men say about foreign women?)

They say, "Farang women, big smelly pussy! Too fat! Too much hair! Breasts long. Not faithful."

(would you advise a new girl that being a bar girl is a good or bad job?)

I don't say. Somebody like. Somebody not like. I want five million baht then I stop work. I have house, buffalo, but now I want money because I want to stop work. If farang send money, maybe not too long work. Maybe two years more work because I have two people sending me money now.

(who is the boss, you or the customer?)

For me 80 per cent, for him 20 per cent. But I make them feel like the boss so I get more money.

(what are problems with this sort of work?)

Sometime girl has fight with boyfriend. Sometime girl no have money. Sometimes girl think about family. Sometimes go crazy for love. But not me. I never care. One, my girlfriend, killed herself. Hung herself. She had the same name as me. She was on pills and ganja. Crazy. Thinking too much. Look on the hand (she displays her wrist), see slicing like this (she slices her wrist with her finger nail). But what can I do? I think like this: when I have good money, big money, I stop.

(any other problems?)

Crazy man want make love like here (she points to her rear). I say cannot. I not like boy.

(would you like to go to a foreign country, maybe Europe?)

I afraid. Maybe somebody sell me. I not sure. If I get married, I go.

(any unusual customers?)

Some man, very nice man, big money, want some lady pee pee and he drink and girl hit him with shoe while he masturbate. No make love, he masturbating. Three girls, only one man. (she then explains something, gesturing obscenely, but the music in the bar is too loud to hear her.) He didn't want girl to touch him. I don't know why. Very nice man. Stayed very nice hotel. We kicking him with shoe on. I worry about him, bloody mouth, very nice man. When he came to the bar, he never looked at girls' faces, he only look at girls' shoes (she points to stage where a handful of girls are dancing in high heels). 5,000 baht each girl. I went with him three times. He wanted me to piss on him so I drank a lot but I couldn't do it. He from America, 28 years old. No letter. Nothing. I'm worried about him because why? Why? I don't think he's crazy. I don't know. The lady boxing him. We pity him. (she kicks fiercely while explaining and pointing to her solar plexus.) One girl hitting him while one girl jumping on his stomach.

(do foreign women come here?)

Farang girls come in and look at the girls and buy girls. I cannot. Sometimes husband comes in with the wife and takes a girl out for three. I cannot eat pussy because I girl, she girl. I cannot.

🐸 🐸 🐸

My Darling,

As I write this letter to you my heart is so heavy with a very deep sadness, that I can hardly see the page that I write upon.

What I am about to tell you makes it very hard for me and I know will hurt you very much. But remember that I love you so very much and dearly with every fibre of my heart.

Darling the decision I have made makes me so unbearably unhappy and very sad. My darling please forgive me. I cannot send you any more money and believe me it hurts me very much to have say this.

The reason I do this is because I have much financial problems in Australia and have to start a new life for myself and to do this I need everything that I earn to achieve this.

126

I am a very lonely and unhappy because of this fact. I have to get a new house because I have given my ex-wife all my property with the divorce settlement. I did this so she will always have a roof over her head. I also have my family to care for if need be. My second son I help very much because he cannot get work in Australia at this moment.

Darling I will never stop loving you and one day in the near future I still wish to marry you. I know this must hurt your heart very much, because I know that you love me.

I cry very deeply to think that the only way we will ever be together is for me to do this to you. I do not know what you will have to do to make a life for yourself, but remember whatever you have to do please be aware that my "love" for you will never "stop."

Darling I do "love you," for deep in my heart the yearning for you will never cease.

Please do not think of me as a cruel man for what I am doing to you, for I know in the long run it will be better for both of us. Darling my love if you have to do what you have to do please be sure my love for you is forever and ever till I die. But that will be a long time to come yet.

Darling I will not telephone any more but will always write letters of love to you. I hope you still love me after you read this letter.

Be sure of one thing. I will try to get to Thailand and see you and apologise to you for what I have done.

Please do not hate me darling because I will always love you. And I am going to marry you when my life is complete and can support you properly and with the respect you deserve.

I hope to do all this as quickly as I can and I want you to wait for me. My love for you is so big that more and more tears come to my eyes.

I will always love you my Tiny Darling and cherish you within my heart. I will always wear your necklace around my neck and kiss it fondly whenever I can.

Please do not be sad and keep in touch with letters for I will write to you every week to express my deep love for you and the sorrow for what I have done to you.

I do this for love darling because if I do not do this there is know way known that I would ever be able to bring you and our daughter to Australia to live with me.

I am so unhappy that this has happened but I truly have no money.

Please keep in touch if you love me for I will always love you and write to you, even see for holiday if I can.

Darling my love gets stronger and stronger for you every day because I will not forget to remember you as I hope you don't forget to remember me my love.

Please forgive me darling but remember I do truly love you. I write to you soon. If you do see my friend he will tell you how much I love you.

Yours Forever.

≈ ≈ ≈

Darling,

It must be 1.10 AM in Bangkok, and I am thinking of you. You must be sleeping now (I hope...). It is 7.10 PM in France, and I am sitting in my office at the end of a long working day, and feeling very lonely, missing you so much. I will soon go home, but nobody is waiting for me there. So I will cook myself a lonely meal, and maybe watch TV a little, and think of you a lot. Why can't we be together?

My friend asked me last Friday for your address and telephone number. She might call you shortly, maybe. She likes you very much and anxiously looks forward to see you again soon. She was in Italy with her friend a couple of weeks ago and wished you were there too for shopping!

How are you, my love? Is everything going all right? I hope I will get some news from you very soon. I know it is not easy for you, because you have to have your letters written by another person, and that it does cost money, but it makes me so happy to get a letter from Thailand! Every morning when I walk out to work, I look into my mailbox, thinking "Maybe today I will get a letter from her!" because it is such a great happiness to get one...

How is your health? Is it getting better? Have you asked your doctor about the name of your disease? Remember I need this information for a more efficient cure on my side, because I do not show any obvious symptom, and I would like to get a treatment if necessary.

My sweetest Thai lady with the most lovable smile, I love you forever and will never let you down. I am really longing for the day when we shall meet again.

Many kisses and lots of love from your faithful Frenchman. Think of me sometimes!

ೋ ೋ ೋ

Darling,

Now I am in Australia and I have the same feeling than in Bangkok the last days without you and on Friday when I came to say goodbye to you. In this time I saw at first, that it is more than only "I like you." And now I'm sure that it is more, I miss you all the time with a really bad feeling in my body, properly in the stomach. But this situation is getting more terrible because I don't know what is your right feeling about me. You said a lot of times that you like me, also that you love me, but I couldn't see in your eyes, if it was the truth, I hope it but I don't know it.

That's because I said I am crazy, to fall in love to a woman like you. I want you, but my chance is very little in compare to all this other men with their much money. But I will try what I can try so long there is a little hope, and before you don't say "go" or "I don't like you" I fight to get you. So I am. I smelled your wonderful body and I tasted your soft skin and this flavour is in my mind. I don't forget it and I want it back. I said I'm crazy (of you). But I don't want only your body. I want the whole you, the laughing and the crying, to feel you nearby, to talk with you, to be happy and to be sad with you.

Maybe you laugh about this words, but I don't care, I want you know how I see and I feel, and you can believe it, it is the truth. I don't joke or lie in this things. And I wait only of the right signal, of the moment I can believe that you want me, and I start to do what I can to make true, to give us a start for a life together.

I don't know in the moment how this is possible, where we could live how we can make a future together. But I have a lot of plans and the most important plan is for me and my friend a business in Bangkok. We know exactly what we want to do in Bangkok, but I think it is not good to speak about this in a letter. And I don't care about this plans if I think about you and me, I know that it is possible if we try it together, even if I take you with me to Germany, what I really do, when I am sure about your love to me! Can you remember what the old woman who lives at your sister's house near your room said when we visited her? She said I should take you with me to Germany. But at this moment I could only laugh about it, and now I think about to do it, that's why I am crazy, crazy about you.

Sometimes in the night when I go to sleep, I close my eyes and think at you. And I try to see you, your picture, your different looking faces: with colour, with a hat like the pictures I have, with the hairstyle you have at work, the sleepy face you have in the morning when you wake up, when you are angry with a devil in your eyes and when you were telling me, in a sudden moment, that you like me too much.

I cannot see this pictures every time, but sometimes I see you, like in truth. This moments are so beautiful that I get a very quiet and nice sleep. Now, where I am writing this letter, it is no problem to see this pictures but my missing and my love for you without the chance to see you really, to feel you, to touch your skin with my skin, to smell you, to taste you; without to put my hands on your soft body your warm skin to lay my face on the outside of your stomach (I don't know the right word for this part of a body) and hear your inside, to rest in your arms without thinking about anything only being happy and dreamy to feel you and to have you. This not to have is very painful.

I count the days where I can see you back to can get all this wonderful things, I cannot expect it.

I could write side after side full with beautiful things, but every word I write makes my missing and my pain bigger. I love you so much, that I think I lost myself at you and this I didn't want before I know that you really sincere with me. But I cannot stop my feelings. All what I have is now the hope that you wait for me and of course that you love me the same that I you. I hope you like this letter and you believe what I said, also that I really sincere with you. (I wrote two letters before this one but they were too confused and not so nice than this one. I show you this letters when I come back.)

So I send you a lot of warm kissings and feelings with the hope that you can feel them. I love you more than

all other things and I want nothing more than you.
Take care of yourself.

৵ ৵ ৵

Hello, my Darling!

Thank you for your phone call to me, I know it's too
much expensive for you. Next time when I want to hear
you, I phone to you.

When you phoned to me you was not happy I heard
it. My darling if you don't really want to come to me,
you can tell me, I'm not angry, I am sorrowful so much
but I try to understand you. For me it's much easy to
love you a long time, but I also know for you it isn't so
easy "to give really" love to me. Maybe, you think you
come here for two or three month to look only, after
you go back to Thailand, maybe you don't really want
to come here and you want to wait for another man,
please come only to me when you really want to try to
love me. I cannot see what you think but I can see
when you happy or not. I can only be happy when you
be happy too. I want that you know what I think. I
think, maybe we can try to stay a long time together
not only two or three month and I know it isn't so
much easy because we don't speak so good in English
language but we can try to do it about really love.

This is the first time for me to ask a girl, come to me,
come to me so much time and I'm sure also the last
time.

I know, you don't like to talk about AIDS but I must
talk to you. My darling, be careful and believe me, if
you don't need please don't do it.

If you really want to come to me I want to help you
to stop fuck, maybe you can stay some month with
your friend and you can stop your apartment and I
send some money for food and I think don't make big

132

party for your birthday, wait for me, when I stay in Bangkok we can make party O.K. Sure, if you really want me I come to Bangkok after May and I help you to make a good Visa. I think the best Visa you get when you marry me in Thailand. You can go outside and you can come inside to Germany without problem.

I want that you think about this letter and I want that you write some letters more what you really want and what you think about me.

When you phoned to me you asked me, do you already work? I don't know what you think but you can be sure, when I stay in Germany, I work. I'm a German man, I work every day ten hours, only Sunday I stay home. I don't drink too much every day and I don't sleep so much every day because I need much money for my life. I have already worked three weeks and I stop again soon, sure.

But now, I want to know why you are not happy to come to me?

My darling, take it easy to come to me, I help you for everything because I want that you be happy.

I love you so much and I want that you stay with me a long time.

All my love to you

I hope the money arrived you.

≀≀ ≀≀ ≀≀

To my beloved Darling

I am truly sorry for what is happening now, and it hurts me really bad, because I know for sure that it is nothing but another case of misunderstanding. If I understand well, you are currently angry with me because you believe that I might think that you do not love me, but only love my money. This is outrageously ridiculous. How could I be stupid and insensitive enough so to think of such a nonsense? The fact that you can get so angry and hurt about such a foolish idea is itself the proof of the contrary. I can hate money when it comes between people to ruin such things as friendship or love, which are the most valuable human feelings and could never be compared to any material, down-to-earth illusion such as ownership, possession or money itself. But what is even worse is misunderstanding between two people who love each other. Such misunderstanding can generate erroneous and hasty decisions and hence lead both involved individuals into lifelong suffering and regrets, just because pride and self-protection would not allow the controversed point to be cleared.

This is the reason why I want this letter translated into Thai, so you can clearly understand my point, which might be vital to the both of us: I swear that I never had such a foolish, insane idea. You have given a wrong understanding of some words I may have said with a totally different meaning, and the reason of this misunderstanding could indeed lay in the fact that you are yourself insecure about my own feelings towards you.

Darling, I love you, truly and faithfully, and I am afraid I will love you forever. Even if I cannot get in touch with you anymore, even if my reasoning mind tells me to forget you, as an impossible dream should be forgotten, my heart and soul will never forget, and your limpid smile and dazzling grace will ever haunt my memories.

Sweetest lady, I could give my right arm for one of your smiles, like a rainbow enlighting the clouds after a storm. I could give my life for your love. I could be your dog, just to be allowed to look up at you.

Today, I'll go to a temple and open my heart and soul to your Lord Buddha. I will ask Him, if I dare, to calm down your unjust anger, make you happy forever and, possibly, to open your eyes about my true feelings towards you.

If I cannot see you before I fly away to my country on Sunday, or if I cannot have this letter delivered to you by my own means, my friend will hand it to you along with my address, and I truly hope that you will, in time, write me, and forgive my farang's clumsiness and the wounds I unintentionally inflicted to your heart.

Your sincerely loving farang, forever willing to serve you.

I will be back very soon.

ॐ ॐ ॐ

Hi!

I saw your ad in a local paper here, and thought I'd like to write to you. I've been in Thailand several times, most recently 12 months go—and I like Thai girls! Unfortunately most girls I met spoke <u>very little</u> English, so it was difficult to communicate.

I am late forties age group and slim. I own a small but prosperous business here in New Zealand. I also own two nice houses, so I am financially secure. I don't smoke or drink, am easy to get along with. I don't mind if a girlfriend smokes or drinks moderately.

I would like to find a pretty and very sexy Thai girl who can speak a little English and who would like a permanent relationship (possible marriage) with someone like me.

If you presently work as a bar girl in Patpong—that's perfectly O.K. with me—I like that kind of girl!

If what I've written in this brief letter appeals to you, please reply immediately and send me your photo (mine is attached). I will then write again and tell you more about myself.

Yours sincerely.

Hello Sexy Girl!

Now it's the handsome Swedish gentleman who's writing you again. Your answer came very quickly thanks for that, I didn't really count on your answer actually, so it made me very happy. Here's your money, I send you a bit more than 300 baht because you had to wait for it. I think it is around 500-600 baht, OK? So now you owe me a free fuck. Ha! Ha!

Here's a photo of you, a very good one, frankly one of the best photos I have of any girl. You are very, very pretty on it and I'm so proud when I'm showing it for my friends.

I'm working hard now but making very good money so I'm not complaining. I have many debts to the bank but I hope that I will get enough to go to Bangkok soon. But maybe, only maybe I will come already soon to buy shirts to sell in Sweden. It's depends on my friend if he can.

In case I will make it, I'm gonna come and give you some hard time again, does it sounds good? You will love it, I'm sure. Sometimes I feel so sorry for you because I know that you miss me so much it must be very hard to be away from someone you love so much for such a long time. Ha! Ha! Ha!

Found a 10 baht note in my wallet, I give it to you so you have a stamp so you can write me again. I would love to hear from you again soon. I send you a truckload of kisses.

Love.

ぼ ぼ ぼ

Darling,

It was great hearing from you. I could almost see your face and feel your body when I read your letter. How are you able to understand my English? And how do you write back to me? If you wish, I will send you a Thai-English dictionary to help you learn English.

I am coming to Bangkok <u>soon</u> for business. I will stay as long as I can, and I want to spend my time with you.

This time we can spend a lot of time together. We can go out to dinner, lie out at the hotel pool, and spend our nights together. We can also talk about you coming to visit me at my home. I can show you America, and if you come in winter, you can see snow. Nothing is as beautiful as looking out of the window in the morning and seeing the grass and the trees covered with snow. Except you. Maybe I will fly you out here for a vacation. We will talk about it.

Anyway, I miss you. I wish you were lying here beside me in my bed. I have a water bed. I don't know if you have ever slept in a water bed, but it is very relaxing, and very comfortable. If you were here I would kiss you, massage you, and I will leave the rest to your imagination.

I want you to write and let me know how I can find you when I come. I can't wait to be with you. I have known many women in America, but none like you. You are very special. If you have a picture of yourself, send it to me. I will send you a picture of myself soon.

See you soon.
Love.

❧ ❧ ❧

Darling,

Are you surprised to hear from me? I don't even know if you remember me. I was the one who went to the Peppermint Bistro with you and your friend. Do you remember?

I'm sorry that I have not written you sooner. After I left Bangkok, I went to Hong Kong and then to Japan. I have only been back about one week and I have been very busy trying to finish my reports. Are you still taking a bath every night?!!!! I am glad that you gave me your address before I left. When I come back to Bangkok I would like to see you.

How have you been? I have not forgotten you and the things that we did together. I hope that you remember me. I am worried that you know too many men and you can't remember who I am. Would you do me a favor? If you can, I would like a picture of you. If you write back to me, please send me a picture of you.

I hope that you will write me. I have been thinking a lot about you since I left Bangkok. I don't know if this letter will get to you. I will put the address on it that you gave me. I hope that they will deliver it. I must close for now. I am sorry, but I am very busy and I have to get ready to go to the United States next week. I should only be there for one or two weeks and then I will be back in Korea. Take care of yourself and please write me and send me a picture of you.

❧ ❧ ❧

Darling,

I received your letter and was very happy to hear back from you so quickly. I am happy that you received my card I was concerned that you might be away and not receive it.

138

You're right about it still being cold here, it only gets to about 5 degrees in the daytime, I am still not used to the weather but one good thing it has only snowed once since I returned. I wish that I would have stayed with you in Thailand for another month instead of coming back here when I did. You're so warm and lovable and sexy. I think about you often and I miss your nice soft thighs.

Are you trying to get a passport yet? I sure hope so. You could come and visit me for two to four weeks, or however long you wanted to. I am sure that I could arrange a visa for you and your sister as well if she wanted to come over with you so that it wouldn't be so difficult for you. I think that I told you already that the best time for you to come is in June, July or August so I hope you will decide you would like to come for a visit.

I want to tell you that I am sorry for lying to you when I came back from Cambodia and making you angry with me that night at the hotel. The girl in Cambodia did not mean anything to me, but you do, so I hope you have forgiven me.

I hope you are well, and that all of your family is in good health. Say hello to your sister for me.

Please write back and let me know how you are and also if you plan on coming here. Otherwise I will have to arrange to visit you in Thailand in the next few months.

Love.

x x x x x

I still have your black panties to remind me of you.

❧ ❧ ❧

Darling,

Sawadee my good friend, hope everything is well for you. I will be leaving my job in Australia and coming to

Bangkok to live as soon as I can arrange everything in Australia. If I get a job in Bangkok maybe we can share an apartment together and you will not have to work at the Rififi any more.

I told my wife about you and now I am by myself. But I could not live with anyone except you again.

By the time you get this letter my friend should have been to visit Bangkok so I hope he gave you my letter.

Look after yourself.

ঝ ঝ ঝ

Hello you!

I hope you're still fine? I get your sexy photo, very nice smile and sexy body, and I like that happy and good-looking eyes. I don't know if you get my letter yet, if you don't I tell you again that I don't really know when I can go back to Bangkok again, but I hope it will be soon. I want to be together with you again and I think I like you to make some food for me, but I also want you to make love to me, what do you say about that? And if you're really nice I maybe will make some cooking for you. Maybe soon, it will depend on my fucking work. I hope you wait for me. Are you often in Kings Lounge? If so, watch out for EUROPEAN MAN, and if use CONDOM you know, you get it only once. I care you. Believe me.

You have something to tell me, what? You also ask me if I remember that you have a bath with me. I don't really know what you mean. Tell me!

Right now I am gonna listen to some Thai MUSIC and go to sleep because it's late, I start to work early tomorrow.

Say hello to your SON from me, and also your friend. Take care of you!

140

I think about you every day.
I miss you.

                    ❧ ❧ ❧

Darling,

I will take very good care of you, because I love you, so just be patient (wait a little longer) and do not worry. I do not want to see a sad darling when I come to Bangkok next time.

I think I can stay in Bangkok for 3 weeks next time. So we can have a good time together. Also, I try to find a job (work) in Bangkok next time. I want to live and work in Thailand.

Also, darling, do not worry about what you do. Do not feel ashamed. Hubert understands. I know you work in a bar, that is how I met you. It makes no difference to me. I feel love for you so it does not matter. I only tell you about having sex for your own good, because I do not want you to catch a nasty disease. (A.I.D.S. is very dangerous because you will surely die if you catch it.) That is why I tell you about make sure man wears condom. I do not want anything bad to happen to you.

I will send you some little presents soon. I hope you received your koala doll. I sent it in a big box to Rififi Bar. I will try to help you with your bank account when I come to Bangkok—you have only 1 month to wait. Last time I came to Bangkok I had more money. This time I haven't got too much.

But I will take good care of you and help you a little bit. I'm sorry but this is how it is. I still care for you (otherwise I would not be spending time writing to you) and I'm very fond of you. I know we sometimes did not get on well together but I have forgotten that.

I will try to help you as much as I can.

So I say goodbye now with love and I hope to see you very soon.

I should get to the Rose Hotel at about 2.15 to 2.30 <u>A.M.</u> very late Friday (actually in the early hours of Saturday morning). I take off in aeroplane at 4 p.m. from Australia.

Maybe I will be very tired when I reach Bangkok, so perhaps you would like to give me a good massage.

Lots of love. See you soon darling, x x x x x x

🐌 🐌 🐌

My Dearest,

Sabai Sabai! I read your letter today and again it cheered me up. I do look forward to your letters it makes me feel close to you, even if we are thousands of miles apart. I miss you very very much, and I really do think of you <u>every day</u>.

My work has been very boring since I got back, but this week I will soon be very busy. But I don't mind, when I am busy I can forget about being in here, and the days are shorter when I'm working.

I am pleased to hear you're are working as a waitress, I hate to see so many beautiful girls pretending to have fun with horrible farangs!

But things in Thailand are so different, believe me, I do not make any judgements, because I have no right to do so, I don't understand your life, and your situation, the only thing I do understand is your honesty and your love. Darling you have a big heart and I wish you every good luck. I wish I could be with you NOW!

You ask about my family, so I will tell you, it is very complicated. I don't know my real mother & father, I was adopted by new parents, and when I was very young I had a brother, but my mother died soon after.

142

My father married again and I had a sister who I love very much.

Please write and tell me about your family and about northern Thailand. I would very much like to know more about you. I wish you luck and hope all your family are well when you see them.

By the time you leave Bangkok I will have sent you some money (3,000 Baht) which I hope will help you a little.

❧ ❧ ❧

Dear Darling,

I got your letter today. I telephoned today as you asked.

Your friend said you were away probably in Singapore.

You promised me that you would stay at home and look after your daughter.

It appears to me that you have a boyfriend. It also appears that your promises are worth nothing.

Please explain by return letter.

❧ ❧ ❧

Dear Darling,

Got your letter thank you. Please tell me this:

1. What bar do you work? Are you dancing?

2. Why do you say you have my baby in 2 months when I was last in Bangkok before 2 1/2 months?

3. Why do you work in a bar? You promised me you would not do this even if we finished. Your sister does not work in a bar, why do you? Does this mean that all our lives every time you have problem for money you will go with other men for money? Do you think I can be happy knowing this?

143

I hope you answer all my questions honestly.

I am OK now but work hard every day. I hope you don't get sickness from working in bars.

I think about you but am not happy.

P.S. A letter takes 7 days to get here.

❧ ❧ ❧

(A pixy. Short, 23 and smiles easily.)

I five years Patpong. I go to AIDS conferences in London, in Victoria Canada, in Germany, in Philippines. I go talking with women working in bar. In Canada they for, government they making, many organizations working for AIDS. Governments. I go with Empower (Thailand's human rights organization helping prostitutes). In group in Canada, I talking what happen these people have AIDS from Thailand. If people have AIDS, we not safe. If people have AIDS, government say take care and check everything. I tell, I go talk with high school and university. They know about AIDS but they don't be afraid because they don't have so much AIDS. In Thailand, if someone have AIDS, have to go hospital or some people have to go to jail. Police take there, stay there. And no see family. Police look after everywhere you go.

(do you tell your audiences that you also work as a bar girl?

Not many people know I work in a bar, because we want to talk about AIDS in Thailand. We not tell, "I come from the bar." We only say, "We know about women work in the bar, we know." When many women work together, we tell, "I work in a bar." But not tell a high school.

144

We have two girls from Zambia and one
Canada, her brother die of AIDS. I be guest. And
from Zambia she got AIDS. She tell what she
Thailand, in Patpong, before they not afraid. B\
they afraid AIDS. Now AIDS more important. Th_y try
to understand. Some people don't think about that.
They don't care. But something changed. New people
came from their country. They heard. Maybe they afraid.

(what do you say if your customer refuses a condom?)

If I tell customer, "Use condom" and they not use, I
don't know how to do. I lose money. But now I heard
many women say, "Use condom." If customer not use
condom, woman not do. If now, I think I leave. If sometime
we need money, I think it very difficult for girl to say no.
Too difficult. Men they say, "If I need condom, why I take
you? I not need you." Mean if I tell customer, "Use
condom," if he need condom, he not need woman. Maybe
he not like use condom. Some people say, "Not feel
good." Some people say they no work when they use
condom. Not like. Not feel to make love.

(do you believe the letters you receive?)

50 - 50.

(have you fallen in love with any of these letter writers?)

I have before. Finish. Some people have wife. They
love me. They not real. Some customer never have girl
before. They see me. When they go back, they have girl.
Too difficult to believe. Many girl get marry. They know
man only two week, three week. They get marry. Maybe
they see man only two, three days and say, "OK, stop
work Patpong" and they take care man.

145

(what do the men say about their foreign girl friends?)

Some man say, "Big girl" or "fat girl." Maybe they make joke. I don't know. They say, "I like a Thai woman better."

(do you know anyone with AIDS?)

I never know, but I heard about the girl have AIDS because we have a meeting about girl have AIDS. But I not go because I have customer. Now AIDS no good.

(what advice about AIDS would you give a new bar girl?)

If she talk to me, I tell something about AIDS. We check with government, government come in the bar, they check blood. They don't tell us I have or not or any girl have or not. We never know. They only check. But many girl go test for themselves. 200 baht. The government check two times.

(knowing all this, what do you tell a customer who refuses a condom?)

If I no have money, I think I will do. I don't care he don't use condom.

(how long will you continue being a bar girl?)

I don't know how long.

(is your work ever fun?)

Sometimes fun. When we have customer and many friends come from different countries, or boyfriend come to marry, or old friend here, we don't worry about money. We don't worry we have to work everyday. We stay with the customer. Sometime we have holiday with them. We not work. We go different city. When we go with customer, they pay for food, they pay for everything. We OK, don't worry, like getting fun.

(and when it's no fun?)

No fun, we not get much money and many people have a problem of their family. Some girl have two children, three children. They very worry. Have to send money, have to send school, buy book.

(do some customers want something crazy?)

They want to make love my ass. I say, "No, this is not for make love." I take off clothes. They don't understand. That he don't stop. He still want to make love my ass. He put me down on the bed and say, "Stay here." I say, "OK. I let you make love my ass. You take shower. I stay here." When he go take shower, I take clothes and go out hotel. He say he not like me, but he like my ass. Very funny. I tell that girl in Canada. Because she ask me, "How do you do if you see crazy man?" You look man first. If the good man, bad man.

(what do you think of Empower?)

I like Empower. I learn speak English in there and I know many things more than before. I think Empower is good place for woman like us. Like me. Many girl can never write Thai, speak English. Can go there. For me, if have some place to go. Some girls they afraid to go office. But to Empower everyone can go. I know, I understand how people. I have been many countries and I have learned more. Like I'm from a poor family. When I'm in Philippines, I know they poor the same. When I in Canada, I see many girl work like me. But more difficult than me. If they have to work on the street, they have to stand up on the street in the cold. Here in the street is not cold. They have to buy more coat.

(what future would you like to see?)

I want fair for woman, everything fair. Maybe fair more than men.

❧ ❧ ❧

Dear Darling,

Money for December.
Also for teeth.

love.

❧ ❧ ❧

Hello,

You dream of my sleepless nights,
To get your wonderful letter was the best and most beautiful thing that is happened to me since I am in Australia and without you!
I never thought that you really send me a message from Bangkok, so I was even more happy standing at the post office without many hope to hear something from you, but the postman gave me this letter, thank you very much.
I think often of you and I miss you every day, and because I think that you don't wait for me, or you don't

sincere with me I get sometimes a very bad feeling, sometimes I could cry. I don't know why, but I love you so much since I met you in this bar and spent all this more nice or less nice days with you.

You said this one terrible sentence in your letter: "I am a lady from a bar and I think that nobody sincere with me."

I understand exactly what you mean, but I don't care that you do this job in this Rififi bar, I met you and I saw that I like you very deep in my inside, so I really sincere with you—I want you and if you want me I take you out of this bar!

I don't know how difficult it is to do this, but I know that it is possible if we both—you and I—try it together.

❧ ❧ ❧

To: Siam Bayshore Resort Hotel

Can you please tell the girl, she has to go back to Bangkok today. I have to be alone the last days I am here. Say she is a lovely girl and I love her. And can you tell her, I will send a check to her from Denmark for about US dollars 100-200. She can buy a present or what she like. She don't speak English. And I need her name and address for the check.

Thank you very much.

P.S. She check out 12. a.m.

❧ ❧ ❧

(At 30, her looks are already starting to fade, but she is still attractive. Her hair is thick and long, flanking high cheekbones as she smokes a cigarette. Wearing a T-shirt with the sleeves rolled up to her shoulders and jeans cut

149

to short hot-pants, her eyes harden whenever she scans around her in the coffee shop, searching among the faces of other bar girls and customers.)

(do you believe the men who write you love letters?)

No, never, because he just play around with me. I feel it. Because everything is not coming true from the heart. Because I stay with him and I not feel it. Not every man. Some is OK.

(do some love you?)

I think for sure. One he say he love me very much. I think for sure. German. We three years together.

(does he love you?)

Yes because we go to the embassy and we going to get married later. Embassy says OK, I can get a passport also. So we happy.

(how are foreign boyfriends different from Thai boyfriends?)

Farang boyfriend is more easy life. Farang has more money. Lady like me, a prostitute, can't get a very good Thai man. Just a boy driving a motorcycle or no good work. There's just no love to the lady. He just want the lady to help him make money. If I stay with Thai boy, I never go to big hotel eat food, or go holiday. Never.

(how did you start as a bar girl?)

First I working in department store. Then I change work. Selling tickets for airline to farang. Start to know

150

farang. I start to speak English. Then I work bartender at Superstar and every day farang say, "I like you." But I don't go with him. Every day I see girls, oh, make good money. This 10 years ago.

(what was it like your first time sleeping with a customer?)

In the beginning I feel a little bit scared. Afraid of a man I never know before. I go with him. What will happen? What to talk? What do do? How can you have a feeling when you don't know the man? After it is OK. For sure it's bad, but it's for the money. Bad for the body. Bad for the heart. Or sometimes you fall in love with man. But it's for my living.

(how do men of different nationalities act?)

German style very bad. Treat lady no good. Japanese man OK. American (laughs), American man think they very high up, very big power. They think what they talk, what they do, is OK. But sometimes it's no good. One American man have very good style, suit, necktie, go in the bar, look like a good businessman. I go with him to Hyatt Hotel. I go in room. I take off my shoes and I want take off my clothes. He say, "No, no, no! Take off your shoes but don't take off your clothes! And come with me." I say, "Why?" He take me walk, walk, walk to swimming pool. Then walk, walk, walk back to room. He say, "Lay down on the bed." He starts licking my feet. It's tickle. I think if he do just this, OK. Something more strange, it no good. But then he play with himself and that's all. Two thousand baht, short time, just to lick my feet. This is my story of American man. Sometimes farang crazy. With another farang I just lie down on back and he write on my back, "Fuck me my daughter" and then fuck me.

(why do some foreign men fall in love with Thai bar girls?)

Because Thailand have a very good heart, very good take care and the man fall in love. She tell him anything to fall in love. But when the man go away, he doesn't know what she do. She say, "I not butterfly. Send me money." Farang man say, "Farang lady don't take care. Big hole." Like that.

(do bar girls lie to their customers and say they love them when they really don't?)

Some lady is true, some lady is not true. I not say "love" for money. When I write, I say, "I think of you very much. I cannot forget you. You are always in my mind. Send me money please, I have a problem." It's the same story. No, it's not true. So now I have the black heart. If this man send me some money, I say, "Thank you. Very good." It means he worries about me. But when I talk with my friend, "My man send me 10,000 baht! 20,000 baht!" it's just to show off. If man say, "I love you but I don't have money for you," I don't believe that. He's just playing around and he don't want to do anything. When he send money, he has some feeling. Maybe not love, but he cares. Now I dream about find a very, very good man who is true to me because it's all bullshit. I don't care about he's a rich man. I can work as maid. Now I'm 30 years old. It's time to stop. Now I feel be good to a man now.

(do your parents know about your work?)

They don't know. I tell them, "I'm a guide." They believe me.

152

(what would happen if you tell them the truth?)

Very bad. In Thai society they lose face.

(what is your opinion of the foreign men who you see in the bars?)

When they're in their country, they can't get a girl friend. They're very lonely. Work, work, work and come back home. When I see them in the bar have a drink, they want to play. In Asia, in Thailand or Philippines, they can get a lady to be with them.

(are you in love with a foreign customer now?)

Today no love. One man, German, I start to like him but it's a problem only for 200 baht. I stay with him not for money. I stay with him because I like him. It start just two weeks ago. I stay with him every day. Eat seafood. Go see boxing, ringside. He spend for this no problem. I am happy. I think this man is good heart. One day I come to see him and he get angry because I late. I have to make a phone call to my momma. I need 200 baht for this. I don't want to ask but I have to, because I stay with him one week. I have no money. He has to understand me. I don't want to talk this (she starts crying). I ask him, "Can I have some money?" I say, "Want go post office." He say, "Why?" I say, "You fucking big farang! You think you can say, 'Do this, stay here!' You think you think you fucking big farang!" He get angry. He think I say, "Please, please stay with me." No, no, never.

(have you ever been to a foreign country with a customer?)

Went to Germany. I don't like it. Near Switzerland border. He have big house and two cars. Very boring. I think these people very rich.

(what do you think about while making love with a customer you don't like?)

I think, finish quickly please. Finish quickly.

(do you hope to fall in love with a foreign boyfriend in the future?)

No more fall in love because now my heart is closed. I have the black heart. Other bar girls talk about, "Man, oh he good," like it's funny. I feel no good for a farang. I feel they just play around. They just have a holiday and they go back home and forget.

(what about the ones who send money?)

Maybe they don't forget. They come back and spend time with lady. But for me, I don't want to love no more. I just take the money. I just like him, but not love. I see many many playing around and so I just want to play back. Because if I broke my heart, who can help me? One girl, she jumped from a building to kill herself because her English boyfriend go away. I see so many girl cut arm because they angry about the man have other lady. But me, I never like that because I love me more than man.

(are most of the bar girls in Patpong happy or sad about their work?)

I think they very happy. (Imitating a bar girl's voice): "Hello? Buy me a drink? You want me?" They just pretend. But some young lady don't think about future. They just think money, good time. Old bar girls thinking of future, want to marry good man. I now walking around looking for man. Not easy to get. Just getting older and older. Now never can save money. It's too small. Before I could save money because I work every day in the bar. 2,500 baht in one day. Sometimes 5,000 baht. Now one week maybe 3,000 baht. Sometimes one week 500 baht.

❧ ❧ ❧

Dear Darling,

This is my first day back in Riyadh and I cannot stop thinking about the way we parted. I'm writing this letter so that I can say some of the things that should have been said in Bangkok.

When you act as you did on Thursday I change from the guy that loved you for so many years into somebody that only wants to escape. You have done this many times and it has never done you any good. My reaction has always been the same.

You know already why we must part. Too many lies, deceptions and scenes like that on Thursday. When I needed to feel proud of our relationship you were slowly destroying it and almost everyone who knew us both could see it happening. There was only one possible outcome but you were blind and could not see what you were doing.

If it hadn't been the girl in the other country, it would have been somebody else. If I didn't have that other Thai girl now I would eventually have somebody else. By the time I went to the other country you had turned my heart against you but it took me a long time to realise this. I needed the kind of love that I gave you. It was never there.

Now you have your business and have a chance to make a success of your life. You have a chance to turn your back on Patpong and all the misery and sickness that can go with it. Also you can learn from your mistakes and make somebody happy.

I am going to try and make a life with the other Thai girl. After my experiences with yourself maybe I'm crazy but I love the Thai people and cannot believe that all Thai girls act dishonestly. The past has of course affected me and I will not give her the number of chances that I gave you but I am happy that I have her and sincerely hope that what she says is what she means.

The Buddha that you gave me is in England but I promise that I will return it to you. If in the future you move you better let me know.

Today I received the tape you sent and have been playing it in the car. Thank you darling. I also like the two songs that you mention. One of them seems to suit our situation perfectly. You know which I think.

I don't want you to think that I feel all cool and clam about our breakup. I have felt very emotional since I got on the plane to come back here. Yesterday and today I have been very upset. You have been Thailand to me for so many years. We shared great moments, happy, sad and funny. These moments are part of me now, part of what I am and to that extent you will be with me always. Should we meet in the future we should smile small smiles and remember those moments and maybe be greatful for them.

Goodbye "My Tee Rak of so many years."

ॐ ॐ ॐ

My Darling, Number One, My Beauty,

I receive your nice letter. I was very sabai and sanuk.

When I see the lipstick in your letter, I make quickly tchak waho.

I come back for 3 months soon. I rent apartment with TV, coffee shop. No more hotel.

Be careful for V.D. and AIDS. Check very good pussy before I come back. Go to the hospital and ask to check your blood. I want to see certificate from doctor. I pay the bill. Don't forget.

I have too much business. I don't drink nothing in my country.

I promise that we going together to Pattaya and Surin.

Don't forget to say "Hello" to the cashier, Mama-san, and friends.

Kiss and Love.

🐦 🐦 🐦

Dear Darling,

I received your letter today. The second letter since I came back to Riyadh. Thank you for the tape.

I can understand that you're hurt and disappointed that things didn't work out for you and me but why are you writing letters like this?

You know very well that I always tried my best for you. For most of the time we've known each other it was me, much more than you, that tried to make our relationship a success. Now you tell me I'm bad, you threaten me and tell me I can't marry who I choose.

I've known the other Thai girl since last year. As I said in my previous letter if it hadn't been her it eventually would have been somebody else. What exactly are you asking me to do now? I should finish with her and come back to you? Do you think that would be any good for either of us?

Darling, life is the strangest thing. Once I wanted you more than life itself. At that time I couldn't have you one hundred per cent and you never allowed me to trust (sy chai) you. Now it is you that wants me but all the broken hopes for so many hears have changed my heart. <u>Does this really make me bad darling?</u>

Why couldn't life have been kinder and allowed us to want the same things at the same time? If I knew the answer to that I would be a wise man instead of just another fool stumbling through his life the best way he can.

Of course I'm not able to switch off my feelings like the light (fie). I think of you in the fondest way. Sometimes I want to cry for what we have <u>both</u> lost. Yes I have lost just the same as you. Now I'm starting again at the same place I was so many years ago. So many lost years darling. You also will start again, that is life, it's inevitable. I do hope that we have learned something from our beautiful failed love my dear.

I don't know what more I can say to you darling. I've opened my heart to you in this letter. As I write everything is blurred because of the tears filling my eyes. I don't think I can ever love that way again. It's tragic that we have lost so much.

When I came to Thailand this time I thought that maybe if we married things would change and work out O.K. When I said to you in the MMM Hotel that I needed to think, this was on my mind. When I was on my own I realised that if we married all the disappointments of the past would never leave my mind and that I would be committing us for the rest of our lives to a relationship of the past, not a relationship of the present or the future.

I thought a lot darling. I didn't go immediately to the other Thai girl. I needed my mind to be clear about You and Me even though we had finished 5 months earlier.

I can't write a letter to make you feel good. Hopefully though I can help you understand through my letters. Do you really think I wanted to say goodbye to all those years? I'm a lot older than you and have less years to spare. This is why I now need to get my life moving again and this is why I want to try again with the other Thai girl before I'm too old to do anything. Time is still your <u>friend</u> darling but it is my <u>enemy</u>.

I have been your <u>friend</u> (and your lover) over the years. I tried to take care of you, I worried about you and I cared for your happiness. Why do you want to make me an enemy now? Is it because life didn't deal us the cards we wanted? If so can you blame me for that?

Love.

꒜ ꒜ ꒜

(She's big, Spanish-looking with her hair divided into two braids framing her face. Giggly and a bit chubby, she comes across as if she has a proverbial heart of gold. Though worn, she's still cute, especially if the light in the bar is just so.)

Me, I am 48 now. Before I good girl. I marry America. Married my age 18. Four year later divorce. Then I 22. Have one son, he stay with my husband. Husband he give me almost one million baht when divorce. I like gambling. I begin bar girl when 28. When I like someone, I do. When I no like, no can do. Money cannot buy me. I play gambling. I stay alone. When I have money, I do everything. After that, I no have much money. I lose my gambling. After that, I sell my house. No have money.

(how did you meet your husband?)

My brother go school United States. My husband, he be good friend. He good job. He work. He business.

(after your divorce and you became a bar girl, what was it like in those days being with American G.I. military servicemen who were in Thailand because of the Vietnam War?)

I have fun. I go for nothing. No need money for me. If I want, I love him. I need money, but if I no like him, I no need. If I love, I want, I like. I no go with G.I. I go with Air America. Pilot.

(why did you prefer Air America, which was the airline in Southeast Asia operated by the CIA during the Vietnam War?)

Air America better than G.I. He like a civilian. He live good. He have room upstairs, very high class. Because he not G.I., he have more money. He live good. He good looking! For sure! I want, I do sometime with officer. Captain, lieutenant, manager, OK. But he gentleman. Gentleman, right?

(did you ever have any boyfriends from the CIA itself during the Vietnam War?)

Before, CIA I have a lot. He give me money. CIA gave me. Me spy with him. For him. But he don't want to show off CIA. He tell me, but no show off. He say, "That one. Ask him." Something he want to know about man in bar. Want me ask him questions. "Name? Come from? What he do? How long he stay here? Real name? Last name?" He give me a lot of money too. He do something bad. I scared I die. Want me ask, "Where he come from? What he doing?"

(after your divorce, did you ever fall in love again?)

160

One time. This guy, no have job, because have big problem with family. Have to go back America. I stay with him three year. Love with him three year. He go back. No come back any more. After that I have no one. He supposed come back. No come back. He had fire in his house, United States, his father died. So he go back. I no love any more. I no want any more. I hurt.

(how many men have written you letters?)

Many men. Someone ask me marry again. I don't want because I don't love him. I cannot go. One America, one Holland. Both send me letter, send me some money. I need money, but I no love them. I think I no happy when I stay with him. I no can live with him long. A week, two weeks, OK. After, I'm tired of them. I don't want to go everyone. Some take me out for dinner. Young guy too. Yes, still do! Sometimes. Now I have some money. He say I old but very pretty. I look like European girl. I very tall. Five-foot seven. He say I 30 years old (she laughs).

(what do you think of the new, younger generation of bar girls?)

Different. Different. No same before. Now they're very very young bar girl. Act not good. Some Thai bar girl have Thai boyfriend. 50 percent. Have work, get money for Thai husband. Give husband. She take care everything. Never have in my life. Farang now is stupid because he don't know she have Thai boyfriend, Thai husband. She not love, only money. Not love. For sure. She have money, like a playgirl. Buy a medicine, she stoned. Before, no have medicine like this. Now have a lot. You stoned like a beer. Capsule. My time, no problem. Now everybody have problem. Big big problem. Medicine number one problem.

(can foreign men marry Thai bar girls and live happy ever after?)

Any farang reading this book, I want to tell the man who want to marry Thai girl: You want to marry Thai lady? You have to meet family. Take time. Be careful. Need money. Have to take care family. Every month. Have to do. He have to pay. He have to send money home. Not the same like America family. Now you have to pay. Have to take care family with money. Ask the lady, "OK, how much I have to give you for family, for mother, for father?" Money. He have to pay more than 10,000 baht a month. 10,000, 20,000 baht. Because of this, they fight, they marry, divorce a lot. Maybe if a farang know this, read this book, he get afraid!

We originally intended to include in this book only love letters to bar girls and interviews with them.

But we were also given letters from the women to men, and have selected a handful of these as a glimpse of what replies some foreigners received.

Hello! My lovely,

How do you do? I think you have fine and good feel. I think you very much.

Last week I went to the north about grow rice in my farm. I'll become to a farmer. I'm glad to do it. On Sunday, my brother had the accident. He drove the motorcycle hit a man and a baby.

So, the policeman bring he to the station police. He want some money from me. But now I don't have money to him for my brother to finish. I'm sad and want to take care my brother from the police station.

Oh my love. Please send some money to me. I want about baht 20,000. Please quickly to send to me. I wait and hope from you to help me. Please help me.

I love you. I kisses you. I want you very much. I hope to see you again on July. Please help me, oh my love.

I love and kisses you.

ನ ನ ನ

Darling,

I hope you're fine.

First I think you forget and no answer my letter because I sent it to you for long time, but I no received your letter. I don't know how about you.

When I received your letter I'm very glad and thank you that you like my doll.

But I don't like that you tell I have Japanese, chocolate man.

Never mind! If you think like that so I'm sorry that you think like that. I never butterfly.

I wait for you come back to see me.

It only you.

ઝ ઝ ઝ

Hello dear,

How are you today? I hope you are well and happy. As for me, I am all right. But miss you so much.

I already received your money. Thank you very much. I am very glad that you don't forget me. Every day I am worry too about you so much. Because you don't call me, I wait for your call one month—already darling you make me thinking too much.

And that money you send me it is not enough. Because I have to pay for my room rent and pay for motorcycle too. Darling you know well for room rent I must pay about 2,700 baht. Please understand me and please send to me some more money about 5,000 baht.

Darling I have some problem to let you know. Because every day have raining too much in the north. My house in the north almost fall because of raining. I am so much worry too about my house. And money don't have in hand.

So I must go to work—again. But don't worry and get angry me. I just work—to get salary only. I don't go out with anybody. Darling I tell you everything true. Really I miss you every day and night. Darling remember that, I waiting for you until the last of time. Nobody can change my mind.

Darling—please write to me and tell me everything about you now. Please look after yourself. Wish you the best of everything. God always blessing you.

All my love to you.

৯ ৯ ৯

To You (Very Bad Man)

You Pussy Flash. Not hero.

How are you. I am not broken heart. Because I don't care. Not want you, and lady Thai not want you too much.

You (fuck you). You say today you have lady. I am not you too much. You not man. But I am no problem and not care.

The man very bad (fuck off)

Flash Bar not want you.

৯ ৯ ৯

My Dearest,

I am so sorry to you. I could not wait to get your phone.

I went to country-side. My friend was died. I had to cremate.

Thank you very much for your kind support. I was received money you sent.

Hope you are well. For me and daughter are well.

I wish you call me. I need hear your voice. Please call me again in April 5. I will be waiting to answer your ring me.

Again, please do not be angry me. I am apologize.

Take care. I do love you.

My Dearest Darling,

Greetings from Thai-girl.
How are you? Hope you are well. For me I am fine.
I feel so sorry I send present for your birthday so late.
Hope you do not angry to me and do not blame me.
Forgive me.
I do not forget you. You do always on my mind.
The reason I send it late because I do not have money
for send it. Hope you understand me.
Hope you like a present I send to you.
I will finish now.
Take care your self.

❧ ❧ ❧

(Every bar has a mama-san. Her job is to watch over
the bar girls. A mama-san may display a bossy, deadpan
demeanor, or the intimacy of a friend to bar girls truly
in need. But the bottom line for every mama-san is to
patrol the bar and make sure the women work hard and
the drinkers keep drinking — and customers get most
of what they want when they rent a girl. The mama-
san also makes sure the customer pays the "bar fine,"
which is the 500 baht or so he must pay the bar as
commission when he decides to take away one of their
girls. Though he's agreed to give an additional 500
baht or 1,000 baht or more directly to the girl for sex,
that deal is strictly between the two of them. The bar
fine, however, goes into the bar's cash register. Bar
owners insist the fine is fair compensation because the
bar loses an attractive hostess for a few hours, or possibly
the entire night, and thus the bar's entertainment lure
will be reduced. Or so the claim goes.

One mama-san, who is serious, efficient but friendly, agreed to talk about her work as a Patpong chaperon and the way her bar girls and customers sometimes fall in love.)

In Patpong I work about seven years. But only three years as a mama-san. Now I 27. Before being a mama-san, I work bartender, work everything bar. Bartender before, and then change to mama-san.

(did you also work as a bar girl before becoming a mama-san?)

No, no, no.

(what does a mama-san do?)

My job, take care of lady, if lady have problem. Or maybe customer have problem with lady. I must to clear what is problem. Maybe lady not good, he pay bar fine but she not go. Or maybe she go but she tell lie, talk, "Not sleep with you," and go back to bar. Something like that. Maybe he want to take bar fine back. Sometime I can give him back, but not every time. But I must to know first, what is problem? Lady no good? Or him no good?

(what percentage of bar girls marry foreigners?)

I not sure. Before, have nice lady, nice and good lady, nice girl. Farang come, she a good lady. But not same now. Lady now going around, eat medicine, talk no good. Farang only make love and, "Bye-bye." Not same before. Before, very good girl, and make love and marry, too much. Before, around five years before, I think 60, 65 per cent marry. But now, no. Now, have lady go

167

with farang but not marry. But farang say, "Don't work. I can give you money. Stop work." But not marry. I don't like that. Lady like OK. Five years ago change. Before, five years before, good lady. Nice lady. But now, very young girl. Drink a lot. Eat some medicine now. Crazy. Farang, good farang, don't like that.

(what medicine do they take?)

Medicine, some eat and be drunk. Valium. That's the name, Valium. And some other. Make same-same drunk. Think nothing and crazy. She don't know anything when she do this. Heroin, I don't know. My bar OK, no have, sure. I don't know, some bar maybe have. Lacquer (for sniffing), yeah, before have. My bar no have. I don't like because I know what she drunk. Drunk whiskey? Or drunk medicine? I know, can smell when lady pass. Sure. It's no good. I think you see lady walking Patpong outside, same crazy, right? Before, she work good. She work go-go before. She can speak English. So now, why she crazy? Eat medicine. Some lacquer. Maybe had some heroin. Too much, too much, so make her crazy. Cannot work now.

(have any of your bar girls tried to commit suicide?)

Yeah, in my bar have before. But I tell her, "You do for what? He make, but don't hurt. But you hurt. No good." But she eat medicine. Hurt with Thai boy. But do herself. For what? He don't care. Thai boy. But she no die.

(why do you think Patpong bar girls have changed?)

Lady now not same before. Now very young, and don't think anything, only happy for one day or tomorrow. Not think of the next years. Lady before, she thinking about next year, or two year, three year more, what will happen. She don't like to work Patpong all time. Before, if she have some farang good, she think OK, she can go and marry, good way for her. And about love, yeah she have. If no have love, I don't think she like marry. Maybe not 100 per cent love, but 50 or 60 per cent love. Must have love.

(why do foreign men sometimes fall in love with Thai bar girls?)

Maybe lady take care good, and something he like.

(and why do bar girls sometimes fall in love with foreign men?)

If maybe she like him, he good, can take care of her, or everything can do for her. Money, that too. If love, but no have money, how you can stay together? But she not think about, "Are you rich?" or, "You no rich." But she think, "OK, we must to have money. Pay everything, and eat and something like that." If she love.

(do you like working as a mama-san?)

Yeah. Because I work high up. For me, good. But I cannot do same-same as bartender before, "Hey! Hey! Drink!" Not fun the same like before. Now just take care of myself and look after customer. I like because I must to meet every people. "Where you from? What country? What happen? You come for what? You business? Or holiday?" I like to meet many, many, many people. Good.

(and your salary is OK for you?)

Yeah, OK.

(how much do you make in one month?)

One month, maybe customer give me drink and little tip. But I don't like that. If you like to give, OK, but I never ask. One month from salary, 6,000 baht. OK now. But after maybe more. Like to have more.

(have you ever fallen in love with a foreigner?)

Me? No. Only friend, take care.

(why not?)

I don't know. I tell them, "Just you very good friend." I don't know why. Because I don't like.

(when you meet other Patpong mama-sans, do you talk about your work?)

No, not talk about work. Because every bar's work, we must top secret. Something top secret. Cannot talk. Maybe I go to see, I know her, I say, "Hello, how are you? Everything fine?" Not talk about work. Cannot. Every bar must top secret. Maybe if we go every bar and talk only work, that no good. Bar owner think that no good, if he know. Every bar same. Cannot speak of some lady, or tell about change some lady, or say something no good for bar, something like that.

(what are the difficulties of being a mama-san?)

Not difficult. I can clear the problems. If about me take care of lady, I have talk-talk with lady. OK, I can clear. But if cannot, I just talk with my manager. If I can clear lady, but customer no understand, just drunk, I don't like to talk. I tell him, "OK you talk with manager." Many drunk farang go out, not pay the bill, something like that. Have fight.

(what problems do your bar girls have with their foreign customers?)

When she come back, she talk of the man go with her. Maybe have some sadist. Maybe he fuck too much (laughs). And crazy maybe. Some hit her. Some sadist. And like to do her ass. Something like that. Or in her mouth. If she don't like, she come back, she tell me, "I don't like him. Him like to have mouth and ass. I go. Not make love." If the man come, I understand. I can talk with him. Or maybe no have condom, she complain.

(do customers sometimes demand you refund their bar fine?)

Sometimes he say, "Lady not stay with me. Why? I pay bar fine. I don't do anything, why she go away? I like to take money back." So I look time. If maybe he take her at 1 o'clock, and no come back to complain until 8 o'clock, or 9 o'clock, I don't give him back. Because you take, you pay for one hour or two hour already. Up to you, you do with her or not. Just not my problem. But if lady tell a lie, I can know, I talk. If true, I can take care of her. If not true, I give money back for him. First I must talk.

(when a new girl applies for a job, how do you decide if she should work in your bar?)

First, what shape about skin? Is skin OK? Good? Slim? And milk? "You have baby before?" If have, the milk OK or not? Maybe cannot work. Fat? Or slim? Fat cannot dance. I don't like. If she can speak English, good. Or worked some before. I look the face, nice? When the customer looks, he thinks, "Beautiful? OK." Or, "Not beautiful." And if she never dance before, I don't teach her to, but I speak some lady, she take care of her because new girl. "You can teach her." Lady teach her. Fun together. Maybe if first time lady, I put her with the lady dancing good, so she can try. Or I ask, "Where you work before? What problems? Stop work over there? Why come here?"

(if she never worked in a bar before, what advice do you give her?)

She never work? I say, "Not scared. You know I take care. Beginning, nevermind." One, two, three days she cannot make money. Nevermind. I can take care. She no understand what farang say, so she come back to ask me. I say, "You remember what this means. Remember." She can listen from lady and talk little bit OK. Easy. "Hello, how are you? Hello." Again, talk together. Easy. But some word is difficult. Never told before. Never heard. So she come back to ask me. I can tell her what it means. So she can have more, more, more, more. She learn herself. We have, inside toilet, make-up, everything. Somebody do everything. Make hair, make-up. Only 15 baht. Or maybe I look customer first, he bad or not? Maybe some customer no good. I know every customer. Come to drink? Drink for fun? Or drink for only fuck? Have money or not? I just talk first. I come to say hello. I ask him, "Where you stay hotel?" Ask him hotel first. That's good.

(when you ask a new girl why she wants to start working as a bar girl, what does she usually tell you?)

Maybe have problem with her Thai husband. Or she need something. Or husband cannot give her money more. Or because she have baby, she must take care of baby. Other problem is her family. Mother, father. Her young sister maybe need money for school. I ask her first, why did she come to work? Have problem about money? If she want to have money, she can work. She can do same-same bar girl. She try. Good or bad, that tells later. I can teach her, "You like to have money? You must work. Because if you work, you have money. Finish problem."

(are new girls afraid about being bar girls?)

Maybe shy. And don't know customer. Maybe two, three days she can understand what she do. I talk with her, some joking. I don't know what she thinking. I just come and ask, "What the problem? Money? OK, money we can give. If you need money, want money, I can give 150 baht or something like that." Because first day she no have, cannot make money. And I speak joking for her, "Smile. Don't think about problem."

(in your opinion, is being a bar girl good work or not?)

Some way good. Some way no. Because if she like to work for money, keep money, and maybe two or three years finish work, OK, that's good. But for some, no good. Only, "Have money!" So when she have money, she go drink. Maybe she go some boy bar. And money she give the boy. For what? I tell her, "Why? You

173

work, you want to have money. Money you have from farang, but you pay for the Thai boy. For why?" I think she have some boy she like, or go every night, give some money, give for drink. And maybe take him too. Crazy. So I talk every time. I speak bad, bad, bad about boy bar. "For what? For what? You give him for what? Money? You make, you must to keep. Go bank. Or give mother, father. Because you have mother, father, they have no money."

(do foreign men fall in love with your bar girls and then ask you for advice?)

Yeah. Have. We have one farang, I don't know he crazy or not, but he really love bar girl. But lady don't care. So many time he come, "Mama-san, mama-san, why I like her? Do you think I love her too much? Why she don't love me?" How can I say? Aaaaaaaaaaaaaaaaaaaah, he crazy. So I say, "OK, drink! Forget it!" Him come many time. But now I never see him around. Four weeks he not come. I forget what country he come.

(and do your bar girls also fall in love and ask you what to do?)

Yeah, have some lady talk that. But I know just not love. But she look the farang, handsome man. Talking, joking. Not love. Because if she love, farang marry her already. In the last one year, about seven girls married. Coming soon, maybe four marry. They like to get it. One girl, she like him, but not love. He like to take her Brazil. She talk with me how she do. I say, "OK. OK. You must go first." Because good for her, she can go outside Thailand. She like to learn something about people. I tell her, "It's not sure if the man good or not.

174

Here he comes to talk good and give money and spend everything good." But maybe if he take lady, go, maybe the lady go work for him. So I tell her, "You must take care of passport. Passport you must keep. Don't give him keep because if you have problem you cannot go back Thailand. Some lady don't know, but I teach her how to do. If the man take passport, she cannot come back. And if she have problem, where to go? Embassy Thailand. Embassy take her back Thailand.

(do you think it's good for bar girls to marry customers and leave Thailand?)

Yes, good. If she no have family, no have Thai boyfriend, good for her.

(why you don't want to go with a foreigner?)

I don't know, but I think I have enough my money. I don't want to give my body for some farang for some money. I don't like.

❧ ❧ ❧

Epilogue

By Mrs. Pisamai Tantrakul

(The owner of a modest, one-room typing school, Mrs. Pisamai also translates thousands of love letters for Patpong bar girls—from Thai to English if they are writing to their foreign boyfriends, or from English to Thai if they have received a letter. In the process, she has developed a unique and intimate understanding of their relationships.)

For four years, I translating these letters. I began this shop as a typing school. After six months, there was some girl, she came to learn typing and she ask me, "Can you translate letter for me?" She is a bar girl. I know some English, so I say, "I can do for you." First, I do not charge any fee for translate. But that girl told her friends, many girls, from Patpong. Now for long letter, I charge 100 baht. Or 50 baht for page. But some are very poor, not have money, so I don't charge money. I read it to them. I see many bar girls because they live around here. I pity them. Sometimes I meet the farang. And if I think farang nice, I tell the girl, say, "This man very nice. If you love him, you try." I give them some suggestion about the life. I say, "You have to try. You have to change your way." If they happy, they come back to me and say, "Thank you" and bring some letters to me.

But some Patpong very stupid. Don't want to change their way. They just think about the money. That is very bad. For the good girl and good man, I have to teach the girl. "Take him to Chiang Mai or see the palace and entertain him." She have to go for dinner. I have to teach her what to do when they go out. What to dress. Have to teach. Because if you don't teach them, they suffer if they go to America or anywhere because very different from Thai style. If they good girl, I help to apply visa, help to apply passport. Or she ask me, "What do you think about this man?" She want some idea. But some of the girls are bad and just want money.

If they only want money, they will tell me, "Please try to help me write this letter, write any good thing for me because I really need money this month." I tell them, "Whenever you want to say anything to the man, remember they also have brain." To get money, the girl will say, "my mother sick" or say, "I take abortion" or "father and mother sick" mostly. They cannot pretend about motorcycle accident or any operation because when man come, he will see no scar. Some girl lie and man come and it's trouble. When any girl try to pretend operation, I tell her, "You have no any scar to show him." So she change her mind. She say, "My mother sick. My father sick."

About 30 percent or 40 percent are happy with the new life and their husbands. Some poor, some rich, but most of them are happy. They are good girls. Nice girls. And they can understand the life. About 50 percent can get married and 20 percent of them cannot be happy and they come back again. They tell me, "Very difficult to adjust myself and stay with him." And some get fighting. Many girls told me she doesn't get enough money from husband because she needs a lot of money to send some back to her family and upcountry.

Usually the way it is, the man will support her in Bangkok one or two years. The man will rent a room for her in Bangkok and send 10,000 baht a month or 20,000 baht. But for Patpong girl, 20,000 baht a month is not enough. I don't know why. Then they get married and take her back to his country.

Fifty percent of Patpong marry. Thirty percent of these are happy. If not, they have to pretend because they want to go there and leave Patpong. So they pretend to the husband. But I meet girls mostly want to marry the farang. If they don't want to marry, they won't contact with letter weekly or monthly. If they only want money, they will only write when they need money.

During the past four years, there were some happy marriages. An American, he work at the embassy. Another man work some Japanese embassy. Also director of big German company. Salesmen. Engineers also. Men who work in computers. Many, many captain for airlines. I meet some of them. Or I know when I help the girl with visa. Restaurant owners. A man who is a producer in music. A taxi driver. Some poor. Some businessmen.

I know this because some girls, they call to me. Because when they go there, they lonely. Or come back on holiday, they come to see me. They will tell me, "Now I have a better life, a really wonderful kitchen, a better lifestyle. My husband is very good to me. Take care to me. He take me go to dinner and outside and party. I don't have to worry the future again. I secure." If husband poor, they have to go work in the farm, but not so hard. They say they work and can get their own money. The husband's relatives, husband's parents very good to them. If they do not go out to work, they say, "Now I plant many flowers around our home. Can travel around the country and visit many places." After, they have children and take care.

The unhappy marriages are because very different lifestyle. Husband very strict to them. Husband very stingy. And different food. And some have to go to work, they don't like to work. They want to stay home and spend money. And some are getting bored because in that place are no Thai people.

They happiest in America. Easy to live. And Australia. Norway. I have about 6 or 7 girls in Norway. They are happy. Holland. Switzerland. Belgium.

The countries they unhappy in is Japan. England, because the people are not friendly and look down to Patpong girl if you have dark skin. The girls told me. German also. They are so serious. They don't like to talk to people. And don't like to smile. French very selfish. Italy, the people not friendly and they are very rude when you go outside. Some man touch her. Very rude to Thai girl. Japanese don't accept the girl from another country. Language is very difficult to learn. English is easier than Japanese. But I know a few girls, they can be happy with Japanese husband because they are the new generation. The girls they told me America, they have an easy lifestyle. They can have Thai friend easily, they can contact together.

Some girls tell me, "I want to get money, please help me write letter." But I cannot do like that. Sometime the girl bring the man. Some men don't know about Patpong girls' behavior, so I explain to the man about the trick and how she manipulate. I tell them man, "If you love her, you should know we have some good girl and some bad girl. So you have to be careful. Because you can lose money for nothing. And the girl fly away. So you have to study your girl." Some of the men, I don't think he love. Want girl to be wife or do homework for them. Or they very lonely.

Very few of the man is true love. About 20 percent. The 80 percent is they have many reasons. They want to have a lifetime friend, they want to have a girl stay with them in their country. Girl to take care of the house. If true love, the man can be patient and give money. I think true love is very stupid. Because he can give everything. Buy a house in Bangkok for the girl. Give a car. And girl can get anything she want from the husband. He stupid. But it's true love. But for the other, have their own reason. "You are good, so I love you."

For the girl, she is concerned you have to have some money. Good job. Then you have to be nice to her. Because most girl have very poor education. But think they are very clever. But clever only in Patpong, not anywhere else. The man have to be very patient because sometimes the girl say very stupid thing.

When I started four years ago, about 40 letters in a week. Ten letters in a day sometimes. After AIDS come two years ago, not so many. Maybe four in a week. Everybody worry AIDS. Even they write to teach the girl about AIDS.

For men and women to fall in love in Patpong, very difficult. But possible. When the man go to Patpong, he will see beautiful girl. But beautiful girl in American eyes. But not beautiful in Thai eyes. Maybe dark skin, but he love very dark skin. He take her upcountry or beach. And they satisfy together. And he send money. And come back on the next vacation. And start to support her for every month. Mostly they start with this style. Love is possible, but very few.

When Thais think of love in Patpong, they think it's very stupid. But I think they can't understand about farangs' life, because in America they don't care where you come from. But in Thailand, when I get married, I have to look back his family and education and everything. In Thai society, we care so much about background. Most Thai people don't understand about Patpong girl and farang lifestyle.

I think forty percent of Patpong girls are good. They think about future. They have an idea to leave Patpong if they can. Try to look for a better chance. Some want to have some money to go back upcountry or get an education. For the good girl, she will talk to me about her background. And her idea. And their future. They believe me, and I teach them. But some bad girl tell me, "I want their money. I want to do any way to get money from farang." Some have broken heart. Good girls' families poor. Mostly it's education. In Bangkok, if you don't finish high school or commercial school, very difficult to find job. Have to go to restaurant as hostess and that can lead to the bad job. They don't care about the job. They take money to give parents.

Most of my friends think I'm very stupid to translate or contact Patpong girl. They laugh. Think it funny, very funny. But I tell them, "This is a good chance for Patpong girl to live a good life and I pity them. And this a chance to help them. Because this is a problem of our country. They don't have good education and don't have good chance to go to good school like us, so they very poor." When I see Patpong girl before I do this work, I hate them, I don't want to talk to them because very dirty or action is strange. After I do this work, I can understand more about them and why they have to work in Patpong. Many girls in Patpong are good girls. Good inside.